CONFIDENCE AT WORK

THE HIGH ACHIEVER'S GUIDE TO NAVIGATING UNCERTAINTY

To Monica,
 Teacher and inspiration, there is so much of you in this book.
 Thank you. Claire

Published by
Hybrid Global Publishing
333 E 14th Street
#3C
New York, NY 10003

Copyright © 2024 by Claire Steichen

All rights reserved. No part of this book may be reproduced or transmitted in any form or by any means, electronic or mechanical, including photocopying, recording, or by any information storage and retrieval system, without the written permission of the Publisher, except where permitted by law.

Manufactured in the United States of America, or in the United Kingdom when distributed elsewhere.

Steichen, Claire *Confidence at Work: The High Achiever's Guide to Navigating Uncertainty*
   ISBN: 978-1-961757-66-0
   eBook: 978-1-961757-67-7
LCCN: 2024945924

Cover design by: Julia Kuris
Copyediting by: Sue Toth
Interior design by: Suba Murugan
Author Photographer: Hesh Hipp
Author Website: clearstrategycoaching.com

CONTENTS

Introduction — 1

Chapter 1
Skipping Through Life, at a Cost — 5

Chapter 2
Impact: Know Your Strengths and How They Contribute — 15

Chapter 3
Influence: Confidence in How You Deal With Others — 33

Chapter 4
Influence: Build Your Brand to Accelerate Your Career — 49

Chapter 5
Initiative: Confidence Is On the Other Side of Action — 57

Chapter 6
Time Management for Energy, Balance and Connection — 71

Chapter 7
Listening and Feedback That Build Foundational Confidence — 81

Chapter 8
Innovation: Build Your Team's Confidence and Leverage Their Talents   91

Chapter 9
Innovation: Creating Spaces for Ideas to Emerge   99

Chapter 10
Where Do We Go From Here?   105

Works Cited   107

INTRODUCTION

"Claire, I've left the company."

The message came from Dana's personal email.

Just like that, one of my most talented clients, one who I thought could transform her organization and could define the future of media in her industry, decided she had had enough.

Despite her incredible experience.
Despite the industry awards.
Despite the progress she was making in influencing key voices in the company.
Despite her ambition, her energy, her fearlessness.
Despite the parade of creative solutions she appeared to pull off, even in the face of doubters in the organization.

To be honest, I wasn't entirely surprised. Dana had been fighting the good fight. And she was tired. I wasn't surprised, but I was frustrated. Because it wasn't the first time I'd seen a talented professional struggle. In fact, it seems to be a new norm. The disruption, the rapid-fire change, and the rising tide of uncertainty enveloping even the best companies in America are taking a toll on the engine upon which their success rests – their high-potential leaders.

You know them. You may even be one yourself or wish you were because they seem to have everything going for them. The problem is that, even for the people who seem to have it all figured out, things are not like they used to be.

For everyone today, even the high-potential leaders, the roadmap that used to be a ticket to success is no longer a sure thing. The tight promotion timetable, the thought leadership, and the financial rewards all seem to have become so unpredictable that today's careers are filled with uncertainty. Economic shifts mean that companies can no longer offer pensions, lifetime employment, lots of organic mentoring and plentiful financial rewards. Increasingly, it feels like the guard rails of career predictability are gone. The time-tested, dependable rules of achievement that used to make leaning in such a worthwhile endeavor have been pulled out from under us.

Because the more you lean in, the more it can feel like if you lean too far you'll fall off a cliff. All those things that used to provide a sense of rhythm and certainty are different. Mentors are hard to find, the question of whether to job hop seems ever present, and even though everyone's working hard, why some rise faster seems so random. The milestones that used to be concrete, linear, predictable, and cause-and-effect feel like they've dissolved into mush.

It's jarring to see especially high achievers like Dana stumble, because it means this increasing uncertainty can happen to anyone with ambition today. Where do you find focus when you no longer feel a sense of agency or sense of control over your destiny? This new, unpredictable normal is even reflected in the fact that, for a growing number of managers and professionals, the lure of entrepreneurship actually feels more like a sure thing than the corporate paths that once provided a sense of stability.

As a trainer and consultant working inside Fortune 500 companies for the last 15 years and a coach working with the high-achieving individuals who form the backbone of these organizations, I have seen more and more of these kinds of disruptions:

- Managers don't know what is expected of them and are less willing to take initiative as a result. That hurts their advancement.
- Increasing overwhelm and disruption make work less rewarding and more confusing. That increases burnout and disengagement.
- People's ability to hang in, let alone respond effectively, is being challenged like never before.

In the midst of this uncertainty, today's middle managers are increasingly holding themselves to impossibly high standards. Many were raised by parents who enjoyed successful careers in the 80s and 90s and want the same for their kids. Technology makes images of success and "15 minutes of fame" hyper present. Couple these pressures with the fact that these professionals are often thrust into positions of responsibility without adequate training, and their capacities are stretched to the limit. From the company's perspective, the crucial results that today's high-achieving managers deliver to the organization, critical to continued growth and innovation, are also in danger.

The good news is that there are ways to counter what seems like dizzying levels of disruption and disorientation, to put both the high-achieving managers and the corporations whose success depends on them back on solid ground. My work within the corporate world has focused almost entirely on how to help the middle managers on whom the success of the corporation depends, not only to respond to these challenges and disruptions but to emerge as stronger, more confident, more impactful leaders. So, they not only strengthen their ability to respond to the current disruption but develop new skills that set the stage for even greater success – for themselves and for the organizations they work for.

I have written this book for these skilled, ambitious high achievers and the corporations that depend on them. Its goal is to provide the CEOs, the corporations they run, and the high-achieving managers and employees who work with them with the road map to increased agency and confidence that gives their organizations a huge competitive advantage in the marketplace.

If you are reading this, chances are that you are an ambitious professional in a large, competitive organization. You have the motivation, but you want the focus and roadmap to grow in your career without sacrificing all the balance in your life. To achieve this and make it your new normal, I'm going to walk you through a series of insights and exercises to fortify and restore confidence, impact, and effectiveness. You will gain the tools to:

- Understand what you bring to the table, so you can enjoy more focus and get the recognition you want
- Know the visible (and invisible) pathways to advancement in your organization and your industry

- Expand your network of relationships and manage those (even difficult ones) so you stay on track
- Increase your executive presence so it springboards your performance
- Let go of perfectionism so you can take initiative and stay focused through the ups and downs

These tools, working in concert, are designed from the ground up to give you agency in managing your career and your team. So, you have the focus to be successful and the confidence to have balance in and out of work.

I believe that change is good. And I believe that having the right tools to thrive in a changing environment is possible. Join me in ***Confidence at Work*** as we explore how to shift from a facade of confidence to creating authentic, foundational confidence. We'll look at techniques and insights to help you thrive and enjoy the journey so you can live up to your potential now and in the future.

CHAPTER I
SKIPPING THROUGH LIFE, AT A COST

"When I met you, I thought you were perfect."

My friend Catherine told me this after three months of knowing me in a year-long business coaching program we both were in.

At that moment, there was an awkward silence that I tried to break by saying, "OMG! that's crazy!" I felt all eyes on me. And under the awkwardness, I felt alone, separate. "Here we go again," I thought. I knew exactly what Catherine was talking about because it had been with me my entire life. Once again, without realizing it, I'd been subtly showing off in an effort to be liked. And the things I was doing to fit in had turned against me, so Catherine couldn't really see me.

Catherine was referring to what I call the "confidence facade," a coping mechanism for a lack of confidence. It's leveraging knowledge or talent to build an impressive, inflated outside that completely conceals internal insecurity. That might not seem like a big deal. After all, "faking it 'till you make it" can be a great way to get through moments that are outside your comfort zone. The confidence façade becomes a problem when it becomes a marathon and the new normal.

In the 15-plus years that I've worked with high-potential middle managers, I've come to the conclusion that the confidence facade is everywhere. In an increasingly uncertain and unpredictable landscape, it is also more present than ever. For some, it looks like always saying everything is ok when it's not, as it did for me. For others, it looks like hyper-competence that always edges out colleagues. For others, it looks like "the pleaser," always saying yes, no matter the cost to well-being. The confidence facade inhibits your ability to be vulnerable or ask for help. It can be confusing to colleagues who see you as more capable than you see yourself. It can even erode trust when that gap in perception of your capabilities comes across as disingenuous. The confidence facade makes it hard to be authentic, to feel recognized, or to create healthy boundaries.

The confidence facade had been with me most of my life, always making it seem like I was fine, like I danced through life. As one of my mom's friends told her once, "Claire … she'll always land on her feet." And like most people, as Catherine learned, I wasn't perfect, and I wasn't always fine. In fact, for someone who seemed to have a lot going for her, I was prone to debilitating bouts of insecurity that seriously hampered my sense of agency, my potential, and my results.

When people struggle to find their "True North" in their career, I believe it's actually the confidence facade, which, over time, erodes intuition. You don't trust yourself. To survive, you resort to using external reference points for success and happiness – the right job, the right relationship, and the right situation. Before you know it, you're in a moment from the Talking Heads song: "Is This My Beautiful Life?"

Why does it matter? It matters because today's knowledge workers, high achievers who are particularly vulnerable to the confidence facade, make up more than 40% of the US workforce.* That's a huge number of people working too hard and burning out, only to fall short of their professional potential. For companies, it matters because, in today's competitive and uncertain environment, it's not enough to have talented leaders. To succeed, companies need each of their middle managers' talents, *plus* the advantage that comes from powerful collaboration. They need people at their best.

A GROWING EXPECTATION GAP

So Where Does This Confidence Facade Come From?

The promise of the American Dream has shifted. Specifically, there is a growing gap between what is expected of people, or what *they feel is expected,* and the resources they feel they have to meet those expectations. Consider the "IBM Man." This mid-20th-century professional was usually a white man in mid-career. He had a pension, job security, and lots of layers of management that he could lean on to get advice. He worked in an expanding economy and a narrower labor pool.

The foundations for today's professionals are much less solid:

- We have 401(k)s, which have advantages but are only as certain as one's personal savings discipline.
- We have layoffs and winding career paths. It's hard to relax and "just do your work."
- We work in lean organizations with rotating bosses. Mentoring is hard to find, even while it's more important than ever in our "post-information" age, where you can pursue so many directions, not all of them fruitful.

At the same time, expectations feel higher:

- Bigger and more diverse labor pools – a good thing – have upleveled what it means to be high-performing.
- Instead of a growing economy (and a growing paycheck), there is business uncertainty and wage stagnation.
- Many of today's professionals were raised by baby boomers who unwittingly pile on the pressure with messages about their own success.
- Technology makes celebrities and influencers ubiquitous; feeling like they are "just like us" can make extraordinary levels of success seem attainable, even expected.

CONFIDENCE AT WORK

In the work I've done for the last 15 years, I've observed that the gradual but vast underlying changes to our economy and society have had an enormous impact on talented middle managers. Knowledge workers at the middle management level are under enormous pressure. At the same time, the pressure goes largely unnoticed because, as Americans, we live in a "rugged individual" culture where striving feels normal. Again and again, I've seen managers worn out by putting their best foot forward while they wait for a break.

Today's mid-career knowledge workers are generally high achievers. They are usually college-educated and are in a competitive corporate career. Their aspirations have them consistently stepping out of their comfort zone, which can trigger self-doubt. This is true regardless of whether they were the first in their family to go to college or had a privileged upbringing. And because these managers have high expectations, they may not give themselves grace for how the workplace changes of the last 40-plus years have impacted them and their peers particularly hard. It's easy to feel "less than" while leveraging experience or success to project "better than." Living in this space of comparing others' outsides to our insides can erode confidence, individually and collectively. With these managers doing the bulk of the work and decision-making at their companies, the confidence façade is putting them and the organizations they work for at risk.

A NEW PATH FORWARD

As we enter a period of increasing global challenge, the good news is that it is possible to meet today's professionals where they are instead of managing their development the same way we would have supported the "IBM Man." Companies need the collective wisdom of middle managers and their ability to leverage their experience. This book is about how I built a framework to shift the Confidence Invention from Façade to Foundational in my own life and how I have helped so many professionals do the same. It's about how to recognize the confidence façade in yourself or your team and how to shift to authentic, foundational confidence. My hope is that this book will help you:

- Build foundational confidence and personal agency.
- Gain access to the creative potential in yourself and in others.

- Learn to bring the best of yourself to work and decision-making rather than your hesitant, reluctant, or abrasive self.
- Show up authentic and know how to manage others' judgments and expectations.
- Share concerns and boundaries without seeming "difficult."
- Enjoy being recognized for the amazing things you do every day.
- Know that others rely on you to make their work and life richer, and you feel it in the most positive way.

This book is about why, as an ambitious professional, you can be riddled with insecurities. And how those insecurities negatively affect your confidence, happiness, and success. This book is also for business leaders who are seeking to get more from their middle managers. For those leaders who hire talent from top schools and competitors and want to leverage that talent toward positive outcomes. For leaders who have big mandates and need all the wisdom their middle managers can provide, to innovate towards extraordinary outcomes.

I call my antidote to the confidence facade "I to the 4th Power;" I to the 4th Power is a blueprint for finding success as your authentic self, even when you're faced with uncertainty, and I'll spend this book sharing it with you.

UNDERSTANDING AND OVERCOMING THE CONFIDENCE FACADE

You might wonder where the confidence facade comes from, how it impacted me, even as a young girl, and why its implications are so crucial to managers and corporations in an era when so much is changing.

My own confidence facade came from being raised by high-achieving European immigrants in the United States. My mom was French, my dad was from Luxembourg, and we spoke French at home. In addition to doing well in school, we were expected to project confidence and ease in many different situations.

Navigating the world outside and always having to be gracious was disorienting and exhausting. I was different at school. I was different with friends. I was different in small, imperceptible ways. And it wasn't just being different; it was that no matter where I went, I wasn't good enough. To protect myself, I didn't realize it then, but I learned to subtly show off. People would say, "Wow, you speak three languages! How amazing!" What they didn't understand was that what seemed impressive came with crushing doubt about how to approach just about everything. Just like in the moment with Catherine, I was put on a pedestal and yet I still felt inadequate.

Somehow, I was able to muddle through without anyone noticing until the moment, right when I was about to hit what felt like career superstardom, it all came tumbling down.

FIRED FOR CAUSE AND THE SILVER LINING

In my 20s, the confidence facade was my boss. On the outside, my life looked great. I worked a couple of post-college jobs, went to business school, and, after a challenging job search, landed a job in marketing at one of the world's largest beauty companies. It was French, which made Mom and Dad super happy. It was prestigious, which made me excited and relieved. Within a year, I was promoted. My star was on the rise.

During that time, my boss asked me into her office. She said they were doing a mini reorg and that they wanted me to work with a VP who had requested to move from Sales to Marketing. I'd be taken off the $40 million skincare business and put, with this VP, on the $6 million sun and body business. Of course, it made sense – you can't give a big category to a VP who just changed functions and is on a learning curve. And it should have felt like a compliment, like a sign that I was considered high potential, that they had chosen me to reverse train this new Marketing VP. But from my insecure, self-doubting point of view, I was sure I had been demoted. I didn't have the confidence to speak up, worrying that they would just hear complaining and think I wasn't a team player.

Not wanting to be a bother, I accepted the job with a weak smile. During that time, the department heads didn't check up to see how I was doing because – confidence facade – I looked like I was fine. They thought

I got it and that this was a stepping stone. But because I was quite insecure underneath the facade, I felt abandoned. I was disappointed. I disengaged.

And then I did something really stupid.

I got a call from a headhunter to interview for a job at a big fragrance company. In the first interview, there were all sorts of red flags signaling that I wouldn't be a fit. But I ignored my intuition. The confidence facade's Saboteur had trained me not to listen to it. So, I closed my eyes, put my fingers in my ears, said, "La, la, la, la, la," and took the job.

And two months later, I was fired. Yes, for cause. I wish I could say otherwise, but I was doing a terrible job. To be fair, there was fault on both sides. But had it not all started with my inability to speak up on my own behalf, I could have found a different path at the first organization, where I'd loved the company and the people I'd worked with.

I remember being in a cab after being fired, repeating out loud, over and over, "The professors in business school said you should hope to fail early in your career, the professors in business school said you should hope to fail early in your career …"

Yes, in the long run (the *very* long run), that failure was a blessing. Before I got there, though, I went through a period of thinking I was spoiled and ungrateful. For all the gifts I had in my life, why couldn't I be happy with a job any girl in NYC would love? From this perspective, I couldn't understand the honest mistakes that had gotten me there. I didn't give myself grace. Instead, I was brutally hard on myself.

Thankfully, I had cultivated a reputation for working hard, so I landed a job within two months of being fired. It was a marketing job at another beauty company. Still not the job function I wanted, but it was a safe place to land, and I learned a lot. I also used the next three years to dust off the leadership tools I'd learned in business school. With time, the experience of being fired started me on a path to listening to myself instead of looking for external validation.

I then moved to a sales role at a large fragrance house to get closer to the people-focused work I enjoyed. There, I used the newfound assertiveness I had been working on to build a fantastic relationship with my boss. Together with our team, we increased our account's sales from $2.9M to $14M in three years.

It was an incredibly fulfilling time. And I couldn't help but wonder how someone hard-working, with talent and potential, could have outcomes at such extreme ends of the spectrum – disastrous on one side and fantastic on another. The conclusion I came to is that confidence drives a sense of agency. When you feel confident, you learn to speak up in ways that sound constructive and mature. You leverage appropriate influence so you feel that you are at choice. And you are resilient to the ups and downs of work and career. *This* is the true, foundational confidence that doesn't have to be fake. *This* is the confidence that knows it has the resources to handle whatever situation comes up. The resource you have is not your accomplishments; it's you.

Confronting the Facade and learning how to build authentic, foundational confidence was the silver lining of getting fired. From there, I built a roadmap in the form of four elements that emerged for me over time: ***Impact***, ***Influence***, ***Initiative***, and ***Innovation*** or ***I to the 4th Power***. With that system, you can understand how your strengths have a place. You can be authentic and still have influence. You can transform the Confidence Invention from facade to foundational confidence so that your instincts and intuition guide good decisions.

This book is not a deep study of any one of the tools I share. I've kept it deliberately short so that, with a little knowledge of yourself and a willingness to learn more, you can make changes that will make a difference right away and add more if you want. Know that you can go much deeper with each of the tools. Resources to do that, if you choose to, are at the end.

IT WASN'T JUST ME

In 2010, I started coaching students from elite business schools and realized I was not the only one struggling with confidence. Outwardly, these students also seemed perfect. But in our coaching sessions, their insecurity, which came from a variety of circumstances, would reveal itself. They would share their fears about the future and what was expected. Other times, they weren't as forthcoming, but their insecurity would come out as critiques of their classmates or former employers.

What I saw was the Confidence Facade. They were leveraging impressive exteriors to feel in control. But unfortunately, their efforts weren't working. They didn't feel confident. So, I would say, "You know; you have a 'terrifying' resume ... good jobs, good schools. You are smart, charming and stylish. Has it ever occurred to you that YOU are intimidating?"

Blank stare and pause.

Then, "Huh. Never thought of that."

These high achievers assumed everyone could see their vulnerability and self-doubt. They assumed others saw them as down-to-earth and approachable. They never saw that their wall of effectiveness could be bringing out the insecurity in others.

The *I to the 4th Power* principles:

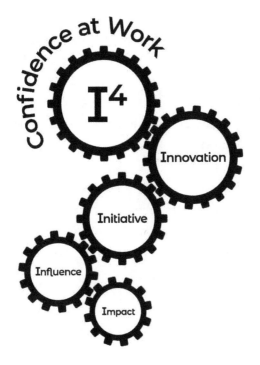

Impact: You hear about strengths all the time. What most people don't do is connect those strengths to their impact on others. When you understand how your strengths contribute to your team and the organization, you have greater agency in how you manage your career and can feel more control over your destiny. That builds confidence.

Influence: When you understand different personalities, you stop trying to be good at everything and learn to be you, and let others be them. You get to be more authentic. Instead of annoying you or threatening you, others' talents become a resource. Together, you can do so much. And knowing how to build trust is at the core of that. Stress levels go down, confidence goes up, and you are more open to feedback that will improve your performance.

Initiative: The Saboteur is the enemy of agency and confidence. Knowing what you are good at is great but growing as a professional and in life inherently comes with uncertainty and risk. Having a tool to help you put the ups and downs into context makes them so much easier. You are resilient, and you don't lose sight of who you are.

Innovation: Most people I know who are in a people leadership position want to feel like good mentors. Innovation is the principle where you begin to pay it forward and use the tools in the first three "I's" to show up as the best version of yourself. You begin to create the "safe psychological space" where Innovation can thrive even in today's uncertain, complex, and ambiguous business environments.

You can read about the four I's in whatever order you like. Again, their cumulative impact is exponential. But feel free to start with whichever "I" intrigues you most. Don't worry about "not skipping ahead," but please do the exercises and practice them with friends and colleagues. Insights are great, but sustained behavioral change requires learning that is on the other side of action.

Now, let's dive in.

CHAPTER 2
IMPACT: KNOW YOUR STRENGTHS AND HOW THEY CONTRIBUTE

> *"It takes far more energy to improve from incompetence to mediocrity than it takes to improve from first-rate performance to excellence."*
>
> ~Peter Drucker

My friend and colleague Cat Williford once asked me, "When do you feel confident?" It's a simple yet profound question. What if, rather than saying, "When I have confidence, I'll be able to do X, Y, or Z," you said, "When do I feel confident, and how do I replicate the circumstances that are present when I feel that way?" This, I believe, is what underlies the Peter Drucker quote above. And so, our discussion of Impact will begin with understanding the link between strengths, agency, and confidence, and their role in dismantling the confidence facade.

A FEW COACHING TERM DEFINITIONS

A few things bother me in coaching and leadership development. The first is that coaches love to give assessments that identify a client's strengths. That's nice, but it's information that can live in a vacuum. The client doesn't automatically know what to do with the information. To have confidence, you must know what you are good at *and the impact it has on others, the work, and the organization.* With that information, it's much easier to connect your strengths to your agency and feel confident about what you are good at.

Another coaching question that bothers me is, "What do you want?" So many of the clients I work with don't know what they want, at least not right now. If you had asked me at age 25 what I wanted, I would have said I wanted to work in marketing at a large cosmetics company, which sounded great. Turns out that was only partly me, the other part was the Confidence Facade. What I find works better is to gain awareness of your areas of strength, connect those to successes you've had in the past, and build from there.

The last question that bugs me is, "What are your values?" Most people respond to that question with things like "honesty," "integrity," or "dependability," which are about ethics rather than preferences. What the question is really asking is, "What are your strengths?" Strengths are the tasks that energize you. They come easily to you. Because of that, you often don't even realize you have them, or you don't know how to define them. Again and again, I've seen clients assume that what they're good at is easy for everyone. Here's the reality: *The things that feel the least like work are where you have the greatest impact.*

Think about that for a moment. Part of why it can be hard to figure out what you want is that it's scary when things don't feel like work. You wonder if you're working hard enough. If it doesn't feel like work, how can you possibly contribute anything? As counterintuitive as it seems, I'll say it again: *The things that feel the least like work are where we have the greatest impact.*

The good news is that the process of figuring out your strengths – what you're good at and want–doesn't have to be long. In this chapter, we'll look at tools that let your unique talents come into view so you can embrace them and stand confidently in them.

I'll share the two assessments I rely on most: the SOCIAL STYLE Model™ by TRACOM and Gallup® Strengths Finder®. I like these tools because they are simple and easy to use at work. Once I've explained these two tools, we'll use several self-reflection exercises to connect the dots.

SOCIAL STYLE® BY TRACOM

When I learned the SOCIAL STYLE Model™ in business school, it was a revelation. For the first time in my life, I understood that different people have different Styles and that *you really aren't supposed to be good at everything*. What I then understood is that you can take charge of your executive presence by knowing which (of your) strengths to leverage in yourself and what to lean on others for.

The SOCIAL STYLE Model is an emotional intelligence tool based on human behavior, that has many applications. In this chapter, we'll use it to help you feel confident about what you are good at and contribute. In the next chapter, we'll use it to help you feel more confident in interactions with others, no matter the context.

Before we can go into defining the strengths of various styles, we need a little setup. The SOCIAL STYLE Model begins with a few principles:

Comfortable patterns of behavior:

- Observing how people typically behave allows you to predict their behavior and adapt to them. The observable behaviors used in the model are:
  - Verbal: Does a person speak faster, more, and louder or slower, less, and more quietly?
  - Nonverbal: Does a person use their hands, lean forward, and make eye contact or do they use their hands less, lean back, and use less eye contact?

CONFIDENCE AT WORK

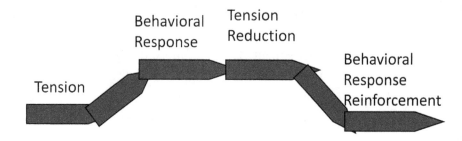

Situational tension:

- Situational tension drives behavior and is normal. When we feel an uncomfortable rise in tension, we have a behavioral response. If that response reduces the tension, it will be reinforced. These behavioral responses vary based on our SOCIAL STYLE and are usually stable by early adulthood.

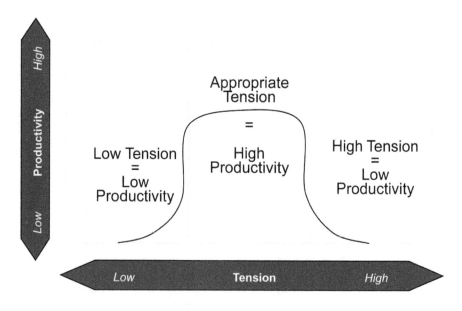

Tension typically drives productivity:

- When tension is in the appropriate range, it feels like high-five enthusiasm, passion for what you are doing, and collaboration with great people. When tension is too low, it feels like margaritas on the beach. Not necessarily bad, but not super productive. When tension is too high because of overwork or tension in relationships, productivity slows down, like a computer with too many applications open.

From here, the SOCIAL STYLE Model defines four behavioral styles by observing behavior and tension on two dimensions: Assertiveness and Responsiveness. In the chapter on influence, we will explore a third dimension, Versatility.

"Say" - Verbal Behaviors

Slower..........Pace of Speech..........Faster
Less..........Quantity of Speech..........More
Quieter.......Volume of Speech.......Louder

Asks	D	C	B	A	Tells

Relaxed........Use of Hands........Directive
Lean Back........Body Posture........Lean Forward
Less.............Eye Contact.............More

"Do" - Non-Verbal Behaviors

Assertiveness: Assertiveness measures verbal and nonverbal behaviors on a "tell assertive" to "ask assertive" scale. If someone talks faster, more, and louder, makes directive use of their hands, leans forward, and makes more eye contact, they are considered Tell Assertive. If they talk slower, less and more quietly, their hands are relaxed, they lean back and make less eye contact, and they are assertive. Assertiveness is measured as A, B, C, and D, with A being the most Tell Assertive, B being mostly Tell Assertive, C being mostly Ask Assertive, and D being Ask Assertive. To understand this more easily, think about people entering a room for a meeting. Who talks first, and who listens first? The Tell Assertive people tend to kick off the conversation. Ask Assertive people tend to take stock of the room and listen first.

"Say" - Verbal Behaviors			Controls / Emotes	"Do" - Non-verbal Behaviors		
Monotone	Task	Facts/Data	1	Less	Rigid	Controlled
·	·	·	2	·	·	·
·	·	·		·	·	·
Emotion In Voice	Subjects of Speech	Form of Descriptives	3	Use of Hands	Body Posture	Facial Expression
·	·	·	4	·	·	·
·	·	·		·	·	·
Inflection	People	Opinions/Stories		More	Casual	Animated

Responsiveness: Responsiveness measures the show of emotion. It measures verbal and nonverbal behaviors on a "controls" to "emotes" scale. If someone has a more even-toned voice, focuses on tasks, facts, and data, uses their hands less, has a more rigid or formal body posture, and a more controlled facial expression, they are considered to Control their show of emotion. If someone has a voice with a lot of inflection, focuses on people, opinions, and stories, uses their hands more, and has a more casual body posture and animated facial expression, they are considered to Emote or share their emotion. Responsiveness is measured as 1, 2, 3, and 4, with 1 being Controls, 2 being mostly Controls, 3 being mostly Emotes, and 4 being Emotes. What's important to know is that responsiveness doesn't measure *how much we feel*. It measures how much of that feeling we reveal. Just because someone seems very poised, think "still waters run deep," it doesn't mean they aren't feeling stress, sadness, or joy.

These two behavioral dimensions define four Styles, which we'll explore in depth now. This is where you start to learn about your strengths and your impact on your team and organization.

Analytical Style
- Slower-paced, slower to act
- Makes strong efforts to organize
- Shows less concern for relationships
- Works in a historical timeframe
- Takes action cautiously
- Tends to avoid personal involvement

Driving Style
- Faster-paced
- Makes efforts to control
- Less concerned for caution in relationships
- Works in the present time frame
- Tends to direct the actions of others
- Tends to avoid inaction

Controls

⟵ Asks | Tells ⟶

Amiable Style
- Slower-paced
- Makes efforts to relate
- Shows less concern for effecting change
- Works in the present time frame
- Shows supportive action
- Tends to avoid conflict

Expressive Style
- Faster-paced
- Makes efforts to involve
- Shows less concern for routine
- Works in the future time frame
- Tends to act impulsively
- Tends to avoid isolation

Emotes

The Driving Style is a combination of Tell Assertiveness and Controlled Responsiveness. These people are typically fast paced. They make efforts to control, which means they naturally take charge. For them, work comes first, and they show less caution in relationships. They work in the present time frame, and they love to be in action.

As leaders, Driving Style people are decisive and willing to take action. They are amazing at execution and moving things forward. They are independent and love to be in action, and to figure things out. For them, stretch goals are thrilling, and they come across as disruptors. They are efficient and pragmatic, easily distilling what's important, and are fearless about venturing into the void and building a roadmap for the way ahead. They are also candid, so you know where you stand. My former business school professor, Bill Klepper has a name for each style. He calls these people the Change Leaders.

The Expressive Style is the combination of Tell Assertiveness and Emotional Responsiveness. These people are also fast-paced. They make efforts to involve others. They are spontaneous, which means they show less concern for routine. They work in the future time frame, often coming across as forward-thinking and creative. They tend to act from the gut and will avoid isolation.

As leaders, Expressive Style people are big-picture and creative, focused on vision. For them, being with people is the ultimate joy. They are enthusiastic, outgoing, and spontaneous. They are often charismatic and easily win others over. They are cheerleaders, like the Pied Piper, getting others on board and broadening the scope of what is possible. They are persuasive – great at selling an idea – and they make things fun. Bill calls this group Vision Leaders.

The Amiable Style is a combination of Ask Assertiveness and Emote Responsiveness. These people are slower-paced. They make efforts to relate to others. They show less concern for effecting change and prefer consensus. They work in the present time frame. They are very supportive of others and tend to avoid conflict.

As leaders, Amiable Style people are natural mentors, focused on people and bringing out the best in others. These people are cooperative and listen, intuitively knowing how to make people feel seen and heard. They are diplomatic, patient, and loyal. They are supportive – experts at creating a safe space where a team can become more than the sum of its parts. They will go to the ends of the earth for their team as long as they feel they are "in a relationship" with their team members. These people can be underestimated as individual contributors but shine once they become people leaders. And they are called People Leaders.

The Analytical Style is a combination of Ask Assertiveness and Controlled Responsiveness. These people are also slower paced, cautious, and slower to act. They make efforts to organize and are drawn to processes. Like the Driving Style, it's work first, relationship second. They tend to work in the historical timeframe, using past performance and results to inform decisions. They tend to avoid personal involvement.

As leaders, Analytical Style people are objective and methodical, focused on leveraging systems and frameworks to create efficiencies that scale the efforts of others and help take teams or businesses to the next level. They measure and categorize so that a team is not constantly reinventing the wheel. They are thorough and "kick the tires" to provide sophisticated, comprehensive solutions and help prevent costly mistakes. Prudent and serious, they are often quiet innovators, finding details that can unleash potential where performance is lagging. They are considered Standards Leaders.

Impact: Know Your Strengths and How They Contribute

For many, four styles can feel constricting, "I don't fit in a box!" That is true; we all possess elements of all four Styles. For most of us, however, one or two of those four styles describe 80% of our behavior, and if you can use the 80/20 rule, SOCIAL STYLE can be a powerful tool.

Which Style, When?

Knowing others' styles, as well as your own, can help you spread the work out across your team's complementary strengths so that, collectively, you have a greater impact. One perspective on this is how the four SOCIAL STYLEs interact in the business cycle, as described in *The CEO's Coach* by Bill Klepper.

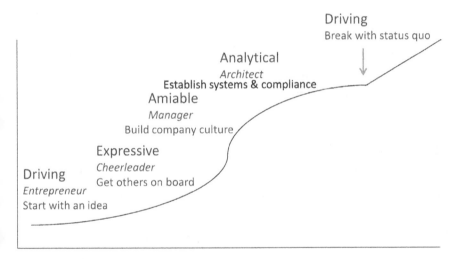

*Klepper, Bill. *The CEO's Boss*

Interestingly, each Style makes important contributions at various points in the business cycle or in a project. Driving energy is very entrepreneurial, starting with an idea. The Expressive energy comes next, as the cheerleader, and gets others on board. Amiable energy is next, as the manager builds company culture and delegates responsibility across a broader team. The Analytical energy comes next, stabilizing the efforts and building an architecture that can springboard the team to the next level. When there is an inflection point because of a large growth in the business or the staff size, the inflection point invites the Driving energy to start the process once more. In a project, a team will cycle through the same energies. In Chapter 3, I'll talk about how to flex each Style to build trust and collaboration. For now, know that we all have the capacity to borrow from other Style energies based on need.

While the SOCIAL STYLE Model gives you a roadmap for owning what you are good at, it also gives you permission to not judge yourself for what you are not good at. It doesn't mean you never have to do things that don't energize you but letting go of judgment can relieve stress. Related to this, the SOCIAL STYLE Model reveals the ways in which others don't always possess the strengths that come naturally to you, so instead of becoming frustrated with a seeming lack of willingness or ability on the part of someone else, you can have empathy. And you can have confidence about your talents and their interplay with the complementary talents of others.

To learn more about SOCIAL STYLE, go to TRACOM.com or read *People Styles at Work* by Bolton.

STRENGTHS FINDER®

The Strengths Finder is another powerful model that identifies your top strengths out of a list of 34. The tool is based on research that indicates that employees are most likely to be engaged when they get positive feedback from their supervisors. It's not surprising that employees are less engaged when they get negative feedback from their bosses. What *is* surprising is that engagement is lowest when someone's boss ignores them completely.

What I love about Strengths Finder is that it gives you a lexicon for talking about *underlying transferable skills*. Not "I am good at Excel pivot tables," which is actually a learned experience, but the thing that makes you interested in Excel pivot tables, which might be "Arranger®" or "Analytical®." Like the SOCIAL STYLE, Strengths Finder can help you align to work that energizes you and where you have a greater impact. It can also help you do your job in a way that is better suited to you. Best of all, once you understand the link between your strengths and your past performance, you can advocate for yourself by linking your strengths to future opportunities. We'll go into how in Chapter 4. For now, let's look at the list of strengths.

The 34 strengths are:

Achiever®	Activator®	Adaptability®
Analytical®	Arranger®	Belief®
Command®	Communication®	Competition®
Connectedness®	Consistency®	Context®
Deliberative®	Developer®	Discipline®
Empathy	® Focus®	Futuristic®
Harmony®	Ideation®	Includer®
Individualization®	Input®	Intellection®
Learner®	Maximizer®	Positivity®
Relator®	Responsibility®	Restorative®
Self-assurance®	Significance®	Strategic®
WOO (win others over)®		

When you know that you have the "Win Others Over" strength, it helps you understand why you are good at client relationship management, don't shy away from public speaking, or enjoy teaching new employees. If you have the "Strategy" strength, it helps explain why getting from point A to point B is like a puzzle that you love to solve. Like the SOCIAL STYLE, Strengths Finder also provides the strengths that do not come naturally to you. And that can also help put those into perspective. It can let you release the feelings of "should" and focus on empowering others to use strengths that complement yours.

STRENGTHS CONNECT TO YOUR PURPOSE

When I started my practice in 2008, I made an important connection: Strengths align with our sense of purpose. At that time, I had clients who had lost their jobs in the Great Recession, and many of them said, "It's been a rough couple of years in finance. I want to have more meaning in my work. Can you help me get a job in a nonprofit?" And in my mind, I heard the needle scratch off the record. *Hmmm*, I thought, *If you spent eight years on the trading floor at Goldman Sachs, you wouldn't last two weeks at Save the Children. The culture is too different.*

What these clients were looking for, I realized, was to be doing work that energized them in their zone of what I call "Skill-based Purpose." It's another term for Strengths. The idea is that there are two kinds of purpose, "Higher Purpose" and "Skill-based Purpose." Higher Purpose is what you think of when you think of Mother Theresa and Martin Luther King. For better or worse, Higher Purpose isn't sustainable if you don't like what you do day in and day out. What most people need is to be doing work in their zone of strengths, which is sustainable, like a well that keeps on giving.

	Purpose		
Experience	Skill-based	Higher	Culture

A client I worked with, Greta, had an MBA and a career in consulting. But she hated the travel and demands to the point where it was affecting her health. We worked together to help her find a new consulting job, hopefully one with a less demanding pace. In the meantime, she had a side hustle as a painter. And because she was very involved in the art scene where she lived, she had direct access to lots of people who bought art.

When we worked together, she would regularly come with fun news. "I've sold another painting!" And another one. And another one. "You know," I said one day, "At this rate, you're going to be able to support yourself with your painting soon." And once she let go of the idea that painting only lived in the "hobby" space, she was able to rebalance her consulting work and make her art a core part of her life. She had more ease and more success.

Hopefully, the SOCIAL STYLE and Strengths Finder have given you a starting point to become more aware of your strengths. Let's now pivot to understanding how those strengths contribute to your team or your company's work. The best way I know to understand the impact of your unique talents is the **Peak Experience exercise*** (see the gray box). This exercise is designed to help you identify the skills and talents that are hiding in plain sight by understanding *the contexts in which they were present* in your life.

HERE'S WHAT YOU DO...

Think of the times in your life, in or out of work, when you were fully alive. You felt strong and powerful, and your fingers and toes tingled with it. You were lost in what you were doing, and time passed unmeasured.

These times can be a period of time, one experience, or an element of an experience. The only rule is that you were doing something you were good at, and something that *you enjoyed*. Good but didn't like it doesn't count.

One note: For this exercise, avoid using vacation, graduation, marriage or childbirth. While it's OK to use experiences from your personal life, those are universal peak experiences and usually mask the underlying strengths.

Think of 20+ experiences. Then narrow down to five to seven experiences.

Once you have narrowed your experiences to five to seven, write the answers to these questions:

- What were you doing?
- Who were you with?
- What was your motivation?
- What did you learn?
- What was your role?
- What was the impact you were having?

> Write your answers in bullet form, or longhand. Once you do this, you will have an extensive list of skills and interests. Now take the list and look for 1) Common threads and 2) What resonates with you most. Remember, you are looking for skills and interests that you were good at and enjoyed doing. **Make a list of the top five, then use the Social Style and Strengths Finder to connect the dots.**

*Adapted from "Through the Brick Wall" by Kate Wendleton and the Peak Experiences exercise from Co-active Training Institute

Why bother to understand your strengths and impact? Because it's the first step in shifting the Confidence Invention from a facade, to foundational confidence. Once you know where you have the greatest impact, you can be so much more effective, with less effort. You can target jobs and projects that align with what you are good at. You can also tweak the job you're in–many roads lead to Rome. Knowing your Impact also activates your Sage, which is you at your best. When you are doing what comes easily, you are more energized, things are more intuitive and instinctive. You come up with more interesting and creative ideas, and you feel more confident to take the risks that can advance your career.

> Another tool I like to use is the Task Inventory. Step one is to make a long list of the tasks you do, daily and weekly. This can take time and fill several pages.
>
> Once you have the list, place the tasks into one of four categories:
>
> 1. Energize and Good at: These are things you are good at and enjoy. They energize you.
> 2. Good at but don't Energize: Maybe your boss wants you to do these, and you're good at them, but they don't give you energy.
> 3. Competent but don't Energize: Again, these don't energize you and you definitely don't excel at them. They probably deplete your energy.

4. Not good at and Don't Energize. These are the tasks to avoid if you can, and certainly not judge yourself for not being good at.

In a perfect world, you get to spend most of your time in the first category, and some in the second. If your job requires you to spend too much time in the last two, do what you can to get a different assignment. You may be able to survive for a while, maybe to gain experience for a promotion, but know that this is not sustainable. Unless your only goal is to make money (and even then), you are likely struggle and burn out.

TASK INVENTORY

Energize and good at	Good at but doesn't energize
Competent but doesn't energize	Not good at and drains energy

IMPACT BULLSEYE

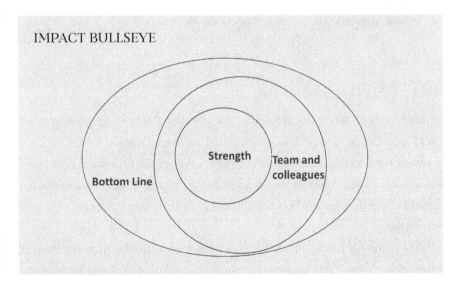

The goal of this exercise is to understand the full scope of your impact. To start, make three concentric circles on a page. In the smallest circle, write a strength that you have. It can be from any of the assessments described above or a strength you've been told about or know you have. Then, think about how that strength contributes to your team. Are you the cheerleader when things get tough? Are you the one who proofreads everyone's presentation decks so you all look good? Are you the one who is undaunted when no one knows where to begin a difficult project?

Next, consider how that strength impacts the broader organization—other teams, the bottom line. Maybe as the cheerleader, you convinced everyone to give a difficult project one last chance, and that saved the company millions of dollars that would have been lost if the project had been abandoned. Or maybe as the cheerleader, you kept everyone motivated so that they did amazing work on a high profile initiative. Maybe as a detail oriented researcher, you found mistakes in a budget that would have meant you couldn't afford key advertising for a launch—and now you can. Or you found a vendor that no one else knew about who was perfect for your team. All of these things can be connected to the bottom line: Increased revenue or reduced cost. Importantly, these are situations where your strength may not be directly connected to the bottom line, but you create impact through others.

RELEASING THE JUDGMENT

In tandem with knowing what you are good at is knowing what you are NOT good at. This is for two reasons: first, as Peter Drucker said, it's a huge waste of time to build a career where you aren't good, no matter how good it looks on paper. And second, you can let go of the judgment about what doesn't come as naturally. You finally realize that *you aren't supposed to be good at everything!*

We grow up hearing that we have to get good grades in every subject. Mom doesn't say, "You know what, sweetie, don't worry about history; just focus on math. You like that more." No! Mom says she wants to see good grades all around. That reality continues through college. Then, the corporate annual review process perpetuates it once more. We learn to skim over the good stuff and focus on what to fix. So, we keep thinking we are supposed to be good at everything.

In my late 20s, I was complaining about balancing my checkbook to a friend at work. How the chore would hang over my head from the moment I finished one month to the moment I sat down for it again. Instantly this friend responded with, "Don't do it!" I said, "What?" And she said, yes, to just not do it. "The bank doesn't usually make big mistakes, and if they do, you'll notice it. Why put yourself through that every month?" A hundred pounds melted off my shoulders, not just because I didn't have to balance the checkbook but because I released the judgment I had carried for not being good at bookkeeping.

When you let go of the judgment about what doesn't come as naturally, you are less defensive and more open to feedback, which means you improve all the time. With all this alignment, you can enjoy more progress in the organization, be more focused and effective, and enjoy work more, which leads to more balance and less burnout. It doesn't mean you'll never have to do tasks you're not good at, but letting go of judgment means you can enjoy the feeling that you are enough.

> I met Anisa at a speaking event I did. She was a little desperate. Her career seemed out of control. She worked really, really hard, and she had had some success, but she had also alienated key people in her organization. Because of that, her career had stalled and she didn't know how to get back on track. We focused on figuring out what Anisa was really good at. After a lot of exploration, a light bulb went off. "I'm a coach!" she said, "My dad was a coach! It's in my blood!" And she got a certification and started taking on clients. Until then, Anisa's career had been like a bouncing ball; with each job change, she seemed to bounce a little lower. Her influence narrowed, her effectiveness was less because she didn't have as many champions in the organization, her reputation

> faltered, and it was harder to get good roles. When she finally made the switch, everything expanded. She showed up confident and was more convincing. Instead of burning her out, her tenacity showed up as courage. She was resilient, and her success turned around. Anisa had been checking external boxes but was in the wrong role.

EMBRACING YOUR STRENGTHS MAKES IT EASIER TO LET OTHERS SHINE

Earlier, I said that the areas where you have the greatest impact often don't feel like work. One really nice side effect of owning your positive impact is that you realize that what's easy for you isn't so easy for everyone else…and that lets you be more generous to others. That grace is super important for working more effectively with others and for leading teams. Another nice effect of embracing your strengths is that it's easier to let others be good at the things you're not so strong in. If you want to get to a leadership position, you need to learn how to contribute according to your strengths, and also activate the unique talents of others. Understanding what different people contribute allows you to deploy them to the right tasks, encourage them according to what's important to them, and expand the scope of your entire team's impact.

I hope this introduction to understanding your strengths, and their impact, has offered insight. The awareness you gain from taking assessments and doing the Peak Experience exercise can be a revelation. And it is, consistently, to my clients. I can't tell you the number of clients I've had who had just never connected the dots. They are performing, but don't know why their boss and the organization liked them so much. They think their hard work is the only thing that's getting them ahead. Once they really understand and accept the unique value they bring, they feel more stable, enjoy greater focus and are less vulnerable to burnt out. They become more effective, more relaxed, make better decisions, and can take on stretch goals and next level jobs.

CHAPTER 3
INFLUENCE: CONFIDENCE IN HOW YOU DEAL WITH OTHERS

When I launched my coaching practice in 2008 I was confident that if my clients just uncovered their "True North," their careers would make themselves. There's more to it than that, as I learned that first year.

In 2008, I mostly worked with clients on job search. The initial conversation with a client went something like this:

Client: "I can't work with that monster/psycho/lunatic one more day."
Me: "Sounds bad."
Client: "It sure is. You've got to help me find another job."
Me: "Happy to help. Keep in mind that a job search usually takes about six months."
Client: "Oh no way. I need a job in the next few weeks. I can't go back there anymore."
Me: "Well, then you'll have to find another coach."
Client: <sigh> "OK, fine, but then you need to give me tools to cope so I can deal with *said psycho*."

So, we used the tools I teach in this book. And I never expected what happened next. Within a few months, more than half of the clients I worked with started saying things like, "Hey, guess what? We were leaving the office yesterday, and my boss told me I'd done a great job presenting to the client! She wants me to present to another, bigger client next week." Huh. Then another one, "Wow. This week, I was expecting my boss to throw me under the bus again in front of his boss. But instead, he let me talk about the status of our project and then said he was happy with the work we'd completed. In front of everyone."

Within a few more months, the same people who'd sworn they couldn't spend One. More. Day. at their job had not only decided to stay, they were either promoted or being positioned for promotion. And over the next couple of years, those same clients saw a second, sometimes a third promotion. In this chapter, we'll look at how those clients gained more control over their work life using influence and how that increased their agency and confidence.

FEEL MORE AUTHENTIC USING BEHAVIORAL SCIENCE

One important way that confidence comes up in my work is when clients tell me they want to be more authentic. When they don't feel they can be authentic, they often chalk it up to confidence. They then see confidence as a hard-to-define, hard-to-attain ideal. What they don't think about is how small adjustments to behavior can help them gain *appropriate* influence. They get better feedback from others, they relax, and they feel more confident to be themselves.

In Chapter 2, I talked about how we are taught to be good at everything. A side effect of that is that so many people get to the work world and don't really understand that different people are motivated by different things, behave in different ways to get what they want, and react differently under stress. What's more, many people judge others' behavior according to the standards of their own Style. Then, they are frustrated, angered, disappointed, or destabilized when others don't follow their rules. And that chips away at their confidence.

Imagine if, instead of feeling anxious about interacting with certain colleagues, even avoiding them, you could feel safe, comfortable, and confident when you engage with them. Everyone has people they get along with easily. But it's often the ones you struggle with that hurt confidence. Ironically, those people are the ones you have the most to learn from and whose interests are most complementary to yours. Here's a leadership hack: It's the people who are the most challenging to you who will do the work you don't like doing! So, feeling more control in your interactions with a greater variety of Styles not only increases your confidence, it lets you expand your influence and impact. Think back to the Impact Bullseye in Chapter 2. You do you, let others do their thing, and leverage it all for better outcomes. As a leader, that's how you expand the effectiveness of your team.

This is what I learned when I first learned the SOCIAL STYLE Model. I suddenly felt like I had Superman's X-ray vision. I could see what people were doing and why. I understood different people's motivations and could see how the behaviors of certain people could irritate, destabilize, or frustrate others, including me. And I could see how the different behaviors could eat away at trust, even when everyone wanted the same big-picture outcome.

Imagine learning the actual science behind your interactions – the rules of why some interactions go well and others don't. Of course, we learn how to behave with others from our parents, extended family, teachers, and friends. But we don't really know how it all works. That means we don't always know how to fix things when they go wrong.

Imagine learning that different people have different behavioral Styles and that evaluating their actions and motives through the lens of *your* behavioral Style can be an exercise in frustration. And that with misguided assessment comes blame, shame, and a loss of confidence. Your confidence.

I recently read about how ancient Greek philosophers decided on measurement – inches, feet, yards. Hard to imagine, but before that, there may have been natural rules about distance, time, or light and dark, but there were no universally understood definitions. The same is true for behavior; just because we can't see it doesn't mean it doesn't have rules. Behavioral models

CONFIDENCE AT WORK

help measure behavior, so you can predict it, and flex to improve relationships and confidence.

FLEX TO BE MORE AUTHENTIC

How well do you know how to deal with others? Have you had people at work who drive you crazy? People who you complain about to your colleagues, then go home and complain about to friends or your partner? Or people you know you need to influence in order to get to the next level but somehow can get traction with? Have you left a job that wasn't working, only to find that you have the same sorts of issues in the next job? Or maybe you just wish you could be more effective in meetings and presentations.

First, be kind to yourself; most of us gravitate to people who share our Style. That means that you can get tunnel vision about how people 'should' behave. It also means that it's normal that work, where you don't get only to work with people who share your Style, can present challenges. Issues around tension that come from different approaches can be improved by understanding the rules of interpersonal interaction. In Chapter 2, we looked at how the SOCIAL STYLE and Strengths Finder 2.0 can help you build

confidence by owning your impact. Here, we'll use the SOCIAL STYLE to learn about Versatility – how to flex to each Style so that you can have better interactions that lead to increased trust and more confidence. To be clear, this is not about *not being yourself*. It's about respecting and valuing what you bring to the table, and respecting and valuing what others bring, then speaking their language while still standing in your worth. The goal is for you to feel calm and confident in how you manage your team and your career.

When you understand how different Styles interact, it is truly like a currency that you can use for influence in so many different situations:

- It helps you build trust and deepen collaboration with your clients, supervisor, direct reports, peers, and other key stakeholders.
- For change and innovation, it lets you tailor messages that make the different Styles comfortable with embracing change.
- For risk and resilience, it again allows you to tailor messages for each Style to help people embrace trial and error and recover more quickly from setbacks.
- My favorite is stress reduction and balance. Remember, once we can let go of the judgment around what we are not naturally good at, we let go of a ton of stress.

If those benefits are not compelling enough, remember simply that each Style brings advantages to a team. Here again are those advantages:

To become more adept at Versatility, we'll examine others' behavior. Doing so allows you to flex to make others more at ease with you and to be less affected by their behaviors that increase your tension. We'll also examine how being aware of your own behavior lets you adjust it according to each Style so that you reduce your behaviors that increase tension for others.

Each SOCIAL STYLE has characteristics:

- Style need is the general goal or motivation of each Style
- Style orientation is the typical behavior used to obtain the Style Need
- Style Growth Action is the behavior that can help each Style communicate and perform better with others

CONFIDENCE AT WORK

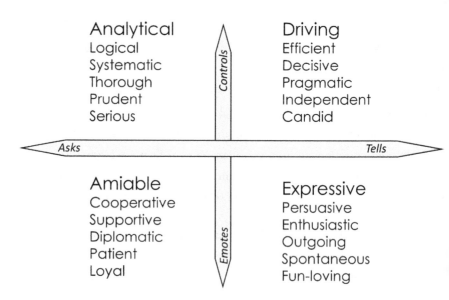

These characteristics are key to helping predict the behavior of each Style:

Style	Need	Orientation	Growth Action
Driving	Results	Action	To Listen
Expressive	Personal Approval	Spontaneity	To Check
Amiable	Personal Security	Relationships	To Initiate
Analytical	To be Right	Thinking	To Declare

Using this chart in conjunction with the Assertiveness and Responsiveness graphs shown earlier, you can estimate your colleagues' Styles and have a shortcut to understand what motivates them and how they typically behave. In Chapter 2 we looked at each Style, focusing on the strengths each brings to a team. Here is a summary again for reference:

If you've made an educated guess at your own Style, you can use these charts to identify your motivations and how you may get triggered when your Style need is at risk or goes unfulfilled. You can also use these charts to know your growth actions – where you can adjust the areas of your behavior that frustrate, confuse, or destabilize others.

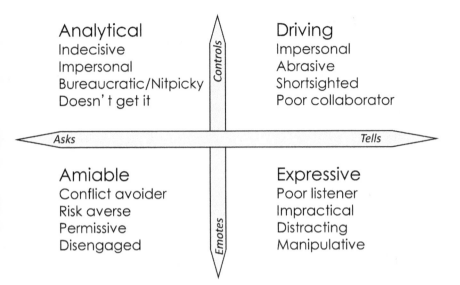

JUST DON'T TRY TO CHANGE OTHERS

As we continue to talk about influence, it's helpful to know how each Style's behavior can be perceived by other Styles as less helpful. The Driving Style can be viewed as impersonal, abrasive, shortsighted, and a poor collaborator. The Expressive Style can be viewed as a poor listener, impractical, distracting, and manipulative. The Amiable Style can be viewed as avoiding conflict, risk-averse, permissive, and disengaged. The Analytical Style can be viewed as indecisive, impersonal, nitpicky, bureaucratic, and just not 'getting it.' If the goal is to increase confidence, then separating others' behavior from your own judgment and giving them the grace of the benefit of the doubt can help you be less affected by their behavior. Knowing how your behavior can sometimes negatively impact others can help you reduce that behavior and also not take it personally if that behavior increases their tension.

Style combinations can be toxic. Each of the Styles shares one dimension with two of the other Styles. But each Style shares no dimensions of behavior with the diagonal Style. And that can be toxic.

To the Driving Style, Amiable people's slower pace can feel like they are not enthusiastic or willing to pull their weight. It can feel like the Amiable Style is waiting for the Driving Style to do the work. That can leave them

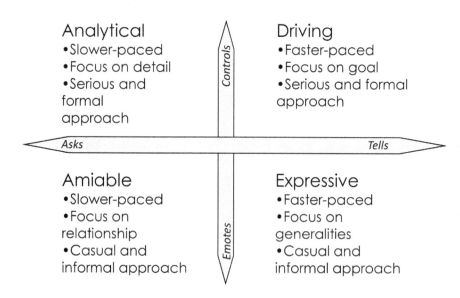

feeling a huge burden of responsibility and like they are all alone. The reverse of this is that, to the Amiable Style, the Driving Style's focus on work and reluctance to engage personally can feel like a kick in the stomach. Also, the Driving Style's apparent ease with managing politics, especially up the chain of command, can seem self-serving and egotistical.

On the other X-axis are the Analytical and Expressive Styles. For the fast-paced Expressive Style, the Analytical pace can feel lost in the weeds. They feel frustrated that the Analytical knows so much but can't seem to synthesize ideas quickly or blend them with the emotional aspects of a challenge. In front of customers, this can be especially frustrating for the Expressive Style. In turn, the Analytical Style can be stunned by how Expressive charm is so convincing to people when their knowledge seems so superficial and incomplete.

And finally, each Style has backup behavior that can be very unproductive. When tension increases, the Driving Style will become autocratic and take charge to reduce tension. The Expressive Style will attack, confront, or want to 'get things out in the open' to reduce tension. The Amiable Style will acquiesce or go along to get along. And the Analytical will withdraw, or shut down, to reduce tension.

Using this knowledge about different Styles, you now know what motivates each Style. With that awareness, you can have more empathy, giving

Analytical

Avoids: Withdraws to reduce personal tension

Driving

Autocratic: Takes charge to reduce personal tension

Controls ↑ | ↓ *Emotes*

← *Asks* — *Tells* →

Amiable

Acquiesces: Goes along to reduce personal tension

Expressive

Attacks: Confronts to reduce personal tension

others the benefit of the doubt. You now also know how your behavior can be perceived by each Style and how to adjust your behavior for each Style. When you focus on reducing others' tension, you increase trust, which helps both people's confidence.

A note on *trust*. You may read this chapter and think, "Why do I have to be warm and fuzzy at work; it's work, after all." Trust has two dimensions: Transactional and Relational, and both are necessary at work. Transactional trust says, "I trust you because you said you would do something, and you did it." Relational trust says, "We're all human, and we're still in a relationship through the ups and downs." Transactional trust is typically more valued by the Driving and Analytical Styles. Relational trust is more naturally valued by the Expressive and Amiable Styles. As we look into flexing behavior to reduce others' tension, remember that adjusting to their preferences around trust is part of the exercise.

> Daniel was frustrated. He was extraordinarily good at operations, and the organization needed his unique talent because they were doubling in size every three years. But as someone with the Driving Style, he was

too direct in his communication around how to reach the team's North Star. He assumed everyone on his team felt the same sense of urgency and didn't take the time to communicate the purpose and goals so that more people would rally behind them. He thought it was his role to know it all and that there was one "right" way to do things. Daniel had to learn to communicate better. Specifically, he had to learn to embrace the good stuff he instinctively contributed and be open to the ways that others delivered on the things that weren't in his wheelhouse.

THE NUTS AND BOLTS OF FLEXING

At the easiest level, Versatility can be leveraged by adjusting your nonverbal and verbal behaviors to mirror those of other Styles. For the specifics of this, refer back to the **Assertiveness** and **Responsiveness** sections in Chapter two. If your Style is Analytical and you are working with someone whose Style is Expressive, then think about leaning forward and using more eye contact. If eye contact is a challenge when you are thinking, then consider preparing for a meeting by thinking things through in advance. Maintaining eye contact will make the Expressive Style person feel more acknowledged and reduce their tension. That will, in turn, make them more present and open to detail.

If your Style is Driving and you are working with an Amiable Style, just slowing down and being aware of your body language that can seem impatient, like a furrowed brow or a lot of nodding to signal "got it!" can ease the tension of an Amiable Style colleague. Body language that seems impatient can make an Amiable Style feel intimidated, which will make them less likely to contribute, leaving you, the Driving Style, feeling like it's all on you. Adjusting to the Amiable Style can make them more likely to meet you in taking charge of an element of the work and moving things forward.

To go deeper into Versatility, consider the Need/Goal and the typical behavior of each Style.

- If you are working with a Driving Style person, keep it professional. Consider proactively sending a pre-meeting agenda. Get to the main points, so keep agenda items down to three or four, no more. And use words like, "decide" and "finalize" rather than "review" or "discuss." Remember that their growth challenge is to listen, so be willing to push back if they seem overly assertive. Always remember to include any relevant deadline dates.

- For an Expressive Style person, be generous with compliments. This doesn't mean being fake; it means acknowledging the efforts of that person, especially where you've perceived value. Be more vocal (interrupting is OK) and engage in "verbal banter" to get a meeting going. Let ideas flow, even if they seem blue sky and impractical, but do paraphrase and reflect, to help this person land or get back on track.

- If you are working with an Amiable Style person, connect first and keep things conversational, not overly formal. Use "we" and "us" rather than "I" and "you." Check in with them personally – this can mean asking how things are going or following up on a personal struggle or success they've shared. Importantly, share something personal about yourself.

- For an Analytical Style person, let them get grounded in the details, and don't get overwhelmed by the amount of detail. Talk less and give them a lot of time to share what they are thinking. When they do, you can discuss or debate but stay focused on the facts. If they need to take the problem away to reflect on their own, be OK with that.

Consider also the backup behavior. For many, backup behavior on other Styles is very off-putting, especially when that Style is a challenge. But here, I would invite you to pause and lean into your empathy. Remember that people engage in backup behavior when they are stressed. If you see a Driving Style person becoming commanding, remind them that you are aware of the deadline and the requirements associated with what you and they are doing. When an Expressive person attacks, acknowledge the emotion they are feeling. You don't have to agree; just let them know you see their upset, frustration, enthusiasm, etc. When an Amiable person agrees but seems reluctant, invite them to share their ideas, and don't hijack them when they do. If an Analytical Style person checks out or stonewalls, slow down and make space to discuss things without emotion. Maybe even put it in writing so they have time to process it. Again, the low Versatility response is to blame others for their negative backup behavior. The higher Versatility response is to offer them grace.

> ### VERSATILITY IN ACTION
>
> What does the SOCIAL STYLE look like in day-to-day interactions? A client, Alex, worked in marketing for a multinational. His job consisted of funneling a lot of disparate details into an effective process, and he was well-suited to it. He liked people, but as a blend of the Analytical and Amiable Styles, he was on the quiet side and preferred to spend chunks of the day working alone. He was detailed and thorough. He was also very thoughtful and had a reputation for being kind to the many people he interacted with to coordinate the details of his work.
>
> Alex's boss could not have been more different. Inspiring but volatile, she had negotiated a part-time schedule so she could spend more time with her family. When the boss was in the office, she often felt out of the loop and behind the 8-ball, which increased her stress. She was like a bulldozer, sharing her frustrations out loud, which came across as attack and blame to her team. She would regularly have tantrum-like outbursts, only to follow those with calm productivity.
>
> Alex was frazzled. He'd lost his confidence and was frustrated. He shared that he dreaded the days when his boss was in the office. He said to me, "Every time she raises her voice, I want to punch the wall. The only way I would scream like that is if the building were on fire. So, I take her at her word, and I can only conclude that I'm doing a terrible job." He added, "What's weird is that right after one of her freakouts, she is totally calm and present like nothing happened. Meanwhile, I'm going for a walk around the block just to keep my head straight."
>
> We talked about different behavioral Styles. I shared that, based on what he had described, his boss was an Expressive. That Style typically

has a lot of charisma and is fun, engaging, and inclusive. The challenge is that they also think out loud. They share the good, the bad, and the unfinished thoughts. What seems like an emotional outburst to others is just a regular conversation to them. And yes, one of the techniques they use to feel calmer and less stressed is to "get it off their chest." Once they do, they feel better…and don't realize what upset they may leave in their wake.

One of the main things Alex could do was to stop taking his boss's outbursts as a reflection on him. Not that his boss's behavior was OK, but barring that behavior changing, Alex could mitigate its impact by not being so affected by it. Next, he could provide his boss with regular summaries of his work. Remember, Alex preferred to work alone and didn't always think to keep others abreast of his progress. His boss, on the other hand, didn't like a lot of detail. Providing his semi-absent boss with short, prioritized summaries could help his boss feel on top of things and would reduce her tension and keep communication more positive. And finally, in a moment when his boss was calm, Alex could find a way to mention that the boss's volume took a lot out of him.

Understanding your colleagues' approach and knowing how to adapt is like speaking other languages. Using the SOCIAL STYLE rules to connect with colleagues above, below, and at your level means that you can enjoy the influence that lets you feel a sense of agency and provides enormous confidence.

In the next chapter, we'll look at how to use the strengths you learned about to more actively advocate for yourself. In the next few pages, I've provided worksheets you can use to practice versatility:

SOCIAL STYLE PRACTICE:

Someone I'd like to improve my relationship with is:_____

In the next week I will probably meet with them: _____

I estimate that this person's style is: _____

Based on that I will adjust the following aspects of my style to resemble theirs:

Posture/stance: _____

Pace and frequency of speech: _____

Volume and variety of voice: _____

Hand gestures: _____

Eye contact: _____

Content of communication (facts/data vs. stories/opinions): _____

_____

I noticed that:

(The following are suggestions. Your impressions are what matters here.)

- The person talked more. They were more actively engaged, and I got a better sense of what they were thinking.
- The person talked less. They seemed less self-centered and I could relate better.
- They looked away more often, so it felt less intense.
- They looked at me more and that felt more forthright.
- Their hand gestures were calmer; they looked more confident.
- Their hand gestures were animated; they felt more passionate and sincere.

Our conversation was more/less: _____

What I liked about that was: _____

If it were like this more often, I think we could: _____

Relationship Map:

Looking at the 5-10 people you work most closely with from your team and other departments, estimate which style each might be. What can you do to flex to their style and increase connection?

Analytical Style

Talks less and more quietly, uses fewer hand gestures, makes less eye contact, is focused on facts and data. Loves to be thorough and think things through.

Who:
_____
_____
_____

What I can flex:
_____
_____
_____

Driving Style

Talks more and more loudly, uses some hand gestures but is also more formal, makes more eye contact, is focused on facts and data. Loves execution.

Who:
_____
_____
_____

What I can flex:
_____
_____
_____

Amiable Style

Talks less and listens more. Uses some hand gestures and acts more casually, makes some eye contact, is focused on relationships, stories, and opinions. Good at bringing out the best in others.

Who:
_____
_____
_____

What I can flex:
_____
_____
_____

Expressive Style

Talks more and more loudly, uses more hand gestures and has a less formal posture, makes more eye contact, is focused on people, stories, and opinions. Very inclusive and enthusiastic.

Who:
_____
_____
_____

What I can flex:
_____
_____
_____

CONFIDENCE AT WORK

My Growth Focus:
Strengths

1. Two strengths I learned about based on my style are: _____
   _____
2. Those positively contribute to my teamwork by: _____
   _____
3. This is especially helpful to the _____
   style(s), for whom these attributes don't come as easily.

Opportunities

1. Two areas that can derail my style when I get stressed are:
   _____
2. The impact on the team can be: _____
   _____
3. This is especially true for the _____
   style(s), who might be sensitive to and/or negatively impacted by that behavior in me.

CHAPTER 4
INFLUENCE: BUILD YOUR BRAND TO ACCELERATE YOUR CAREER

One of the most heartbreaking career stories I've heard was from a professor who shared that when her first child was an infant, she worked long hours, publishing at three times the rate of her male counterparts. When it came time to choose who would get tenure that year, the administration chose a male colleague. Why? Because he had consistently been in the office of the head of the department sharing stories of his successes and talking about what he wanted to accomplish for the department and in his career. In short, he was advocating for himself.

Gender aside, up-leveling visibility can be challenging. If you're like a lot of people, maybe you hope that if you just put your head down and do good work, you'll get noticed. Interestingly, in the classes I teach, I find that it's not so much that people don't *want* to advocate for themselves; it's that they don't want to do it in the ways they imagine it – boastfully and arrogantly. But personal PR doesn't have to feel yucky. In this section, I'll talk about breaking down self-advocacy. I'll talk about how to advocate for yourself in ways that are quiet and specific so it doesn't feel like showing off. And in turn, I'll advocate for practicing regular and consistent self-advocacy. Not only does practicing personal PR help people know about you, but it also helps you feel more confident.

MAKE IT EASY TO ADVOCATE FOR YOURSELF

What makes self-advocacy hard for most people is that they imagine a boastful, obnoxious person talking about how great they are at everything. It's off-putting. And it's even worse for people who are not American-born. I've worked with many multinationals, and what I hear again and again is, "I can't brag like an American." What I always remind non-Americans is that, in most countries, once you graduate from a good school, you are on track to be supported even during ups and downs in your career. For Americans, it's not that way. You can graduate from a top university – you are still only as good as your last good work. That's a tough reality, and it means that you have to be willing to advocate for yourself.

The good news is that there is an easier way. Over the years, I used what we learned in the first chapter on Impact, specifically the Peak Experiences and the Impact Bullseye, to create a tool I call the **Impact Statement.** The Impact Statement is used a lot like an elevator pitch, but it's different in key ways. Most people think an elevator pitch is their resume. They assume that an accumulation of impressive job titles at impressive companies will be evidence of their superior talents. Their pitch starts something like this, "My first job out of college was…" and immediately, the person they're talking to checks their watch.

An Impact Statement is different. It says:

> This is what I'm good at…
> and this is *what I can do for you."*

The statement is not a comprehensive catalog of your strengths and experiences. The "This is what I'm good at" part points to the specific strengths and experiences relevant to the objective. And while it still takes courage to talk about your strengths, it's a baby step compared with, "I'm the best, and I can do anything!"

The "This is what I can do for you" part points to desired outcomes. We'll go a little deeper into this, but for now, know that numbers and easy-to-express positive outcomes get people's attention. The Impact Statement looks ahead to what the person you're speaking to wants and makes the link from past, proven results to future possibilities. And that is critical – when you talk about what you think you can deliver, even the potential for it, you show that you *understand the person's challenges*. You get what keeps them up at night. And by doing that, you demonstrate that you have agency and that you think beyond where you are now. That focus on your audience's needs is key.

I've found that for many of my clients, focusing on others' needs is even harder than talking about their own strengths. These clients don't want to be presumptuous. They think, "Who am I to tell an SVP what they should be doing?" But there's a nuance there. You aren't claiming to know all that they know. You're simply expressing that you understand the challenges they face when working with someone at your level. And having taken the time to figure that out goes a long way.

I once spoke to a recent college graduate who wanted an administrative assistant position with a cosmetics marketing VP.

"I had internships at *Elle* and *Vogue*," she told me, "And I can't get anyone to give me an interview."

"Wow, those internships sound great," I said. "And I'm sure you did a great job. But it doesn't tell me how you contributed."

"I never thought of it that way," she said. But she was ambitious, so she wasn't put off. "Then what should I do instead?" she asked.

"Great question. First, think about the challenges of being a marketing VP. One is that you have a lot on your plate, and time management is always an issue. Another is that it's very competitive, and a lot of senior leaders can feel threatened by colleagues. Try this: 'During my internships at *Vogue* and *Elle*, I noticed two things. First, you have to be willing to figure things out because everyone is so busy. I did that and because I did, I got more responsibilities. And second, I learned that you have to know when to reach out to someone in another department, and when to check with your boss first. So basically, I'll get as much done for you as I can on my own but will check in with you so I don't overstep.'"

"Right. Got it." She wasn't claiming she knew how much of a $10 million budget to spend on advertising versus in-store events. She was simply saying, "I get what a VP wants from a good administrative assistant, and I think I can do that."

An Impact Statement lets you showcase your strengths and accomplishments in ways that are natural and don't feel forced. Yes, you still have to have courage and stand in your worth, but instead of boasting or overpromising, you are just saying what's possible, given what you know.

As important as the Impact Statement is knowing when to use it. Advocating for yourself doesn't work when you do it once a year in your annual review or when you get that one amazing interview. The key decision-makers who can help you (your boss and others) need to know that you are serious and consistent about what you want. They need to hear it again and again. And they need you to paint the picture for them. People can only help you when you give them the message.

HOW THE IMPACT STATEMENT WORKS

Something you are good at (strength)

\+

A result you've obtained (impact)

\=

A desired, relevant outcome for an interviewer, your boss, a key stakeholder, and ultimately, the organization

An example might be:

> "Sally, I'd like to talk to you about my next steps. I really loved connecting with the participants when you asked me to do that training, and the feedback numbers support that the participants really enjoyed my delivery. As we look toward AI transformation, I'd be interested in talking to the head of AI about whether I could join that team in a training capacity. I think if we can continue to engage the AI transition team, they will learn faster, and the transformation will go a lot more smoothly."

Not boastful. Just showcasing a strength or success and linking to a relevant challenge for the audience.

The shorter, more memorable, and repeatable your statement, the better it works.

When I graduated college, I was certain that I wanted to be a perfumer. I wanted to spend my days in a lab creating fragrances. That turned out to be the completely wrong job for me, but what's important is that I told *everyone*. That fall, I was doing temp work as an administrative assistant. I'd tell everyone that I wanted to be a perfumer. It was short, and it was memorable. By my third two-week assignment, one of the admins was in her boss's office and told him, "This girl wants to be a perfumer. Have you ever **heard** of that?"

"Sure!" he said, "My friend Gus is a perfumer. Send her in here. I want to talk to her."

And two weeks later I was sitting in a fragrance lab mixing oils as an apprentice to a perfumer.

The Impact Statement won't always be as short as "I want to be a perfumer," which, incidentally, didn't include anything about my experience. But it should be short and focused on potential.

SHOWCASE YOUR ACCOMPLISHMENTS BY ADDING "WAR STORIES"

Here's the step where you get to talk about all of your rich experiences. Once you get a person's attention with the short Impact Statement, you can back it up with "War Stories," which will keep the conversation going. How do you do that? By using short, memorable stories that build your credibility.

Here's an example of an Impact Statement with backup War Stories:

"Thinking about my next move, I see a couple of options. As a salesperson with good analytical skills, I can help the organization sell complex financial instruments. Or I could help our long-term strategy group analyze consumer trends and prepare us for major market changes."

Here are a couple of "War Stories" that can back it up:

War story 1:
"Last year I was asked to attend a client meeting to explain our product design to this $40 million client that we were at risk of losing. We were able to hold on to the client, and the client has asked me to be present in meetings to brief their tech team ever since."

War story 2:
"For several years, our account managers have invited me to work on their annual business plans. They say that I understand how to help them measure what events are likely and what that might do to their clients' businesses."

What's important about the backup stories is that they are separate from the Impact Statement. I mentioned earlier that most people think a pitch is about "getting it all in." But people lose interest. What works is giving a headline, like those six-second ads online. You want them not to press "Skip Ads," and you do that by focusing on them and their needs. So, when you create your Impact Statement, edit it down as much as you can. Also, edit the War Stories so they don't get too long. Remember to link the War Stories to skills and experience that are relevant to the problems your audience (boss, stakeholder, hiring manager) is trying to solve.

SELF-ADVOCACY IS AN IMPORTANT LEVER

The bigger picture here is that advocating for yourself is a key element of your career. I've heard so many clients express frustration that putting their heads down and doing the work wasn't working, that politics are cynical, or that when someone isn't getting the results they want, they feel the need to go back to school or acquire more certifications. Sometimes, that's valid, but much more often, it's a misdiagnosis. What's really needed is a little personal marketing.

Another important piece of the puzzle is to know with whom to use your Impact Statement. The first time I heard the term *sponsor* was in Carla

Harris's book "Expect to Win." Carla explains that while we would all love a mentor, mentors aren't necessarily the ones who can make decisions on our behalf. For that, you need a sponsor. With mentors, Carla says, you can share "the good, the bad, and the ugly." With sponsors, you share "the good, the good, and the good." When you advocate for yourself, make sure you know who the sponsors are in your organization and that you are sharing your Impact Statement with them.

Bethany came to me frustrated. She was selling financial instruments for a major bank. And she was good at it. Still, she couldn't get the promotion she wanted.

I asked Bethany about how she was as a little girl and what stories her mom used to tell her.

"Oh, that's easy!" she said. "When I was little, if we were traveling on an airplane, I would go up and down the aisles talking to people. Then I'd come back and tell my mom, 'That old lady is going to visit her grandchildren. And that family is going on their first vacation since their little brother was born. Oh, and the flight attendant lives in Spain!'"

Bethany was a people person—curious about them, who they were, and what they were up to. And that's why she was so good at selling. But she had never made the connection.

Next, I suggested that she share that story in her job interviews.

"What?" she said, "I can't do that! They'll think it's unprofessional!"

"Try it," I said. "Your interest in people is the gift that keeps on giving. Salespeople in financial services are a dime a dozen. Maybe people think you're only in it for the money. If they see that people really are your passion, they will trust that you'll continue to perform for their company."

She did try it. And they loved it. They got it, and they got her. That built her confidence. She was offered a stretch job that put her on a whole new level.

Advocating for yourself is an important part of shifting the Confidence Invention from Facade to Foundational. Self-advocacy doesn't have to be boastful. It can be as simple as giving your boss an update about what you did during the week. Use the Impact Statement as a template and do it regularly. Speaking up for yourself takes time and energy, but it does get easier.

CHAPTER 5
INITIATIVE: CONFIDENCE IS ON THE OTHER SIDE OF ACTION

"Life goes in the direction of the conversations you are having – with yourself and with others."
~ Rick Tamlyn, Coach and Author of "The Bigger Game"

The first year of my coaching business, my Saboteur had me in its grips. My mentor at that time, Ron Renaud, told me, "You won't be a coach until you've advertised and delivered a workshop in a church basement for $10 a person." I did that. Then, I did a four-week program at the same church for four participants – $60 per person. It sounds like a cool War Story now, but it didn't feel that way then. It was terrifying. Seriously. While there had been moments in my life where I had taken a bold step, nothing prepared me for the constant fear and taking action that comes with having your own business.

In those early days, my Saboteur was saying, "How is this your life? You went to business school; you worked in Fortune 500 multinationals for 15 years. How are you hustling $10 workshops in church basements? It went on,

"You loser! You could only find two people willing to pay $10 ... to come to your workshop."

I had to learn that these were only thoughts and that, instead, I could tune in to my Sage. She was saying, "Wow! Two people you found on Meetup.com were willing to come to your workshop and share their stories. That is amazing! You are so courageous! People find what you are talking about so interesting!"

The story may seem comical in its extremes—experienced Fortune 500 professional-turned-church-basement-hustler. But I'm grateful for the experience because it taught me to recognize the Saboteur when it shows up in my clients.

I'll say it again about the context that today's middle managers find themselves in. It's a perfect storm of mounting pressure and uncertainty with decreasing support. Taking initiative in this sort of environment requires a lot of courage, but it is critical to your growth.

The Center for Creative Leadership created the 70/20/10 ratio to express that cognitive learning or the powerful insights people gain in leadership training courses, is great but only contributes 10% to leadership development. In fact, 20% of development comes from the support of a good supervisor or mentor. But the vast majority, 70%, comes from putting the cognitive insights into action. That means that if you want to grow in your career, you have to be willing to consistently take initiative. Let's now turn to how to manage the Saboteur and tap into your courage.

> Eva was a classic case of not realizing her impact. She was doing an amazing job. She was considered a prime candidate for senior leadership. But she didn't get that she was exceptionally good. It sounds harmless, but it wasn't. Eva was beyond burnt out. Her stress was affecting her health. One day, I said, "You know, you turned this failing brand around."
>
> She said, "Not at all ... I just did what was obvious. Anyone would have done it."

> And then I said, "Yes, except the three people before you didn't do it."
>
> That took a moment to sink in. But in time, it was like she had found free money in a pocket—this thing that had always been there was now hers. Once Eva really owned her impact, she smiled more, was less intense at work, and her health began to restabilize.

UNDERSTAND THE SABOTEUR

The chapters on Impact and Influence explained the important roles of *self-awareness* and *mastering interpersonal dynamics* in dismantling the Confidence Facade and bringing out your best, authentic self. That state of mind is referred to as the Sage, which I call "Vacation Head." It's the state you're in near the end of a vacation when you're relaxed. You say, "From now on, I'll always have the clarity of mind to know what to do. So-and-so will never drive me crazy again. I'll be able to put down my work each day and go home at a reasonable hour. I've got this." When you are in your Sage mode, you know what to do. You are full of ideas. You're not stuck. You're creative. You come up with solutions, and you make sound decisions.

What gets in the way of the Sage is the Saboteur, and it's always been around. Think back to Greek tragedies; the "furies" were the disembodied voices that kept the hero or heroine from being their best, driving doubt and bad choices. Saboteurs are downloaded into the psyche at a young age. They are a lens through which you see the world, most often tilting self-perception to your disadvantage. This lens follows us through life, which is why success doesn't release you from self-doubt. In his book *The Happiness Advantage*, Shawn Achor talks about how distressed he was to find that half of the undergraduates at Harvard University were unhappy, even depressed. He set out to answer the question of why half see Harvard as a thrilling opportunity, and the other half see it as a trap. Spoiler alert: It's the Saboteur.

The Saboteur shows up in ways that are sneakier than you realize. The Saboteur is present when you say, "I just had a vacation; how can I be tired?"

Or, as I once heard from a job-search client, "What should I say in interviews about that time, 14 years ago, when the promotion I had asked for was delayed by three months?" Feeling like you are lazy, procrastinating, perfectionism, and comparing yourself to others are all signs that the Saboteur is present.

The Saboteur is also the voice that criticizes others: "S/he is so unprofessional" or "You know, we would be able to get all this done if we had a better team." In her powerful book *Loving What Is*, Byron Katie shares how what we criticize in others is actually what we dislike about ourselves. Blame and contempt are ways that we diminish others so that we can feel better.

The Saboteur loves tunnel vision—the feeling that you are trapped, that the current reality is bad and there is no way out. In the *Power of Now*, Eckhardt Tolle points to how we imagine that things will be better when we have a bigger team, a fancy car, or we meet the love of our life. It even says that everything will work when you have confidence; another way to look at the confidence facade. The Saboteur also loves shame; it keeps you from being vulnerable, which gets in the way of the trust and collaboration that build confidence and reduce stress.

What does the Saboteur look like in the workplace? I see three Saboteur-fueled high-performing professionals again and again:

- **Burnt-out**: Maybe everyone loves this person. Maybe they are doing a great job. But getting it all done wreaks havoc on their balance

The
Burnt-Out
Manager

The
Disengaged
Manager

The
Abrasive
Manager

and self-care. Running the career marathon at sprint speed wears them out. They don't see it because everyone seems to support their over-functioning. But that effort leads to health issues, loss of friendships, being overly emotional, or eventually having to quit their job.
- **Disengaged**: This might look like burnt-out but it's different underneath. Maybe this person feels disappointed, resentful, or overwhelmed. Those feelings can be toward people, workload, or the office culture. They don't know how to communicate their feelings, so they give up. Maybe that looks like sliding in at 9:01 and being the first out the door at 5:00. Maybe it looks like not wanting to travel for work or attend company events. At its worst, it leads them to job-hop, which can hurt their career and damage the team they've left.
- **Abrasive**: This is the person who is constantly frustrated with what they see as inadequacy in others. As a result, even though they may be doing good work, their direct reports don't seem to develop. There's lots of turnover in their team, and they don't build robust networks. Conversations that feel direct to them are seen as confrontational by others, and others avoid them.

These profiles are variations on a theme, leveraging talent and impressive qualities to project confidence. They are the Confidence Facade, all fueled by the Saboteur.

GET TO KNOW YOUR PARTICULAR SABOTEUR

To get to know your particular Saboteur, start by exploring the messages that you hear when you are embarking on something new or are feeling uncomfortable or under pressure. Maybe the voice in your head says, "If this was worth doing, someone much smarter than me will do it way better." Or maybe it says, "How can it take you so long to do this? Other people do it so much faster." The Co-active Training Institute suggests describing your Saboteur and asking yourself two questions that I love:

1. What does your Saboteur do when you are not around?
2. What threatens your Saboteur?

The latter one is almost always connected to your strengths and talents.

In the fantastic book *Positive Intelligence* (Positive Intelligence, 2006), author and coach Shirzad Chamine defines "accomplice Saboteurs," which can be another way to get to know your personal Saboteur lens. Chamine points out that there is one ever-present Master Judge, which I call the Drone, and nine Accomplice Saboteurs, which you can explore on the Positive Intelligence website:

- Hyper-achiever
- Hyperrational
- Pleaser
- Avoider
- Restless
- Hypervigilant
- Controller
- Stickler
- Victim

Everyone has a different combination. Once you get to know them, you can recognize them pretty quickly. In fact, you can flip situations so that instead of saying, "I am uncomfortable or afraid in this situation, so that will probably trigger my Saboteurs," you say, "Hmm ... I'm feeling a ton of pressure to get this all done *yesterday*. That's my Restless Saboteur. I guess this situation is stressing me out more than I realized."

Taking it further, the Saboteurs can conspire together, so if you have the Hyper-achiever and the Restless, you may have a bad habit of setting goals that are too big in too short a time frame. Take some time to consider how your Saboteurs might conspire together, and then notice when they do.

> Bethany was one of my earliest clients. Her career had started in the public sector, and she seemed stuck there. She was determined to get into the beauty industry and had a fantasy that once she got there, she would finally be happy. But the more she wanted it, the more nervous she was in interviews. She kept getting first rounds, but it

wouldn't go beyond that. A very loud Saboteur was pointing to circumstances, telling her that if only she had this dream job, she would be happy. In our work, Bethany learned to focus on what she was good at and let the paralyzing fantasy soften. She wasn't just good at corporate communications. She was incredible. By taking on a more visible role in the public sector, she built her confidence. She took a bridge role at a communications agency that exposed her to beauty and fashion clients. And then was offered a senior role in a highly respected company in the art world.

CONSISTENTLY MANAGE THE SABOTEUR

In today's crazy world, with its upleveled expectations and scaled-down resources, the Saboteur doesn't only show up in response to unique or discreet incidents. It's around almost all the time because we are living with stress almost all the time.

In *Positive Intelligence*, Shirzad Chamine refers to neuroscience, saying that when you are in the Sage mindset, you are strengthening positive neural pathways, and when you are in the Saboteur mindset, you are strengthening negative ones. The more you are in Sage thinking, the more you strengthen the neural pathways that help you respond with calm, confidence, focus, and creativity. The more you are in Saboteur thinking, the more you strengthen neural pathways that make you feel doubt, confusion, and hopelessness.

This fascinating science reminds me of something I learned years ago. We are all born with the capacity to learn any of the world's languages. What happens as our parents focus on just one, is that the neural pathways for that language become stronger, while the neural pathways for other languages become weaker. It's why, as adults, it is so difficult to be accent-free in a foreign language. According to Chamine, If you consistently strengthen the Sage synapses, you rewire the brain. That tips the balance away from insecurity and negativity and toward confidence and positivity. Let's look at how to strengthen the Sage on a daily and weekly basis.

Gratitude

In *The Happiness Advantage*, Shawn Achor writes that gratitude is one of the most powerful ways to build your sage. Having a simple daily practice of writing down three things you are grateful for in the morning and at the end of the day increases happiness. It doesn't work to say, "I appreciate my kids, my spouse, and my mom" day after day. What works is writing down three things you are grateful for *from the last 24 hours*.

My favorite form of gratitude is **appreciative inquiry** because it's where gratitude meets Impact, and it is a huge confidence booster. Here's what you do:

1. At the end of the day or the week, look at your calendar and identify three to five accomplishments for the time period. They can be quantitative or qualitative: You reached a sales goal, had a good talk with the newest team member, or waited in line to see the latest Marvel movie at midnight on opening night.
2. Then, for each accomplishment, write your responses to the following questions:
   a. What is the accomplishment?
   b. Why is it important?
   c. What would further progress look like?
   d. What, if any, are the immediate next steps?

It's amazing how this exercise shifts you from feeling like you're dragging behind the eight ball to feeling on top of your game. It is especially powerful if you connect your accomplishments to the strengths you learned about in Chapter 2. When you do that, you reinforce that your success is sustainable.

You can also do this exercise as part of your annual review. For that, select one or two accomplishments for each month, then narrow down to the ones that you found most energizing. This approach to annual planning shifts the energy from "Let's drag everything we didn't get done from last year to this year" to "What if we could reach our goals by following the energy and spending much more time in our Sage mindset, individually and as a team." When you operate from a Sage mindset, you not only enjoy the journey, but you increase overall performance.

One team I did the appreciative inquiry with had generated double-digit growth for three years in a row, but they were exhausted. They couldn't see their good work, so they blamed each other. Once we reviewed their last 12 months through the lens of appreciative inquiry, they were ecstatic. They got back in touch with their collective Sage and were calmer and much more effective.

Classic Self-care

Exercise, enjoying friends, being in nature, and volunteering are tried-and-true classics, as are watching what you eat and drink. These may sound boring, but they go a long way to helping build mental fitness and stabilize mood. Also, schedule your work around your vacations and plan fun things. Anticipating something exciting increases happiness and confidence.

Impact and Influence

Remember that Impact and Influence, the first two I to the 4th Power principles, are also powerful Sage builders. When you use the tools in this book to get the recognition you want at work, it's good for your Sage. The same is true for day-to-day interactions. An interaction doesn't have to be demonstrative for it to build the Sage; it just needs to be positive. What's more, when you stand in your worth by using your Impact Statement (Chapter 4), you also create Sage-building self-esteem.

Feel Your Feelings

Feeling your feelings might seem obvious, but too often, shame interferes with our ability to do that. I remember once sitting on the couch and managing my shame so that I could feel deeply some jealousy I was experiencing. Amazingly, within a few minutes, the jealousy had lost its grip. Once that happened, I was able to recognize the essence of what I wanted and realize that it wasn't so far out of my reach.

In the course he teaches, Cultivating Emotional Balance (healingintoflourishing.com), my colleague Felipe Rocha details the ways in which we avoid the hardest of the seven universal feelings: fear, anger, *and sadness*. He says that fear is associated with potential loss, anger is what we feel when there is something in the way of what we want, and sadness is the universal healing emotion. When you can pass through your emotions, you reduce the power those feelings can have over you. What's more, you reduce the negative compensatory behaviors that the unprocessed emotions can cause. You weaken the Saboteur and regain access to the Sage.

Meditation and PQ Reps

Stepping out of your experience and finding stillness is a powerful way to build the Sage pathways. Meditation, prayer, or time in nature are all valid ways to do this. Again referencing *Positive Intelligence*, Shirzad Chamine recommends small mini-meditations throughout the day. He calls these "PQ Reps." I recommend checking out his book or website, where he describes PQ Reps for touch, hearing, vision, muscle tensing, and relaxing.

Gratitude, self-care, and meditation done regularly, will build the Sage muscle and have a profound effect on mental fitness. You will feel less overwhelmed, stronger, and more confident in decision-making and managing others.

WHEN YOU'RE FEELING STUCK

Now, let's turn to moments that shift the Saboteur into high gear. Maybe you are facing a bigger challenge. Maybe something is urgent. Or maybe you've experienced a failure. For those moments, my favorite tool is the "Perspective Wheel." I first learned about the Perspective Wheel at Co-Active Training Institute. It's fantastic for helping you feel "at choice" and not trapped. When we are stuck, we tend to collapse or mix different perspectives, which makes it hard to make intuitive or well-thought-out decisions. The Perspective Wheel exercise asks you to consider different perspectives one at a time. Another way to think about it is that you are giving voice to different parts of yourself.

Looking at different perspectives does several things, consciously and unconsciously. First, you give yourself and others a break. You're not making excuses. You're looking at perspectives from a place of being human, especially when the situation warrants it. About a year and a half into COVID, my friend Dave called me and said, "I'm losing it. I thought I could keep my cool, but I'm now realizing how nuts it's been and that I'm actually kind of depressed." He really thought he could maintain a cool perspective and stay happy and positive, even in the face of a global lockdown. Don't forget to give grace to others, too. When you are frustrated with someone, it's easy to want to blame them. Consider using the Social Style Model to see things from their point of view.

The next thing the Perspective Wheel does is that it pushes you to ask, "Is it really true?" My friend Teresa Sande asks this question in *Find Your Fierce*, her book about imposter syndrome. When you go for a promotion and don't get it, is it really true that you don't have what it takes or that the organization will never give you the recognition you deserve? Could it be that people get promoted at your organization every two to three years, and you've only been in your current role for a year? Or could it be that you legitimately have a gap in the experience required and that your boss has your back and is working to make sure you fill that gap? This step of exploring the situation helps manage the negative fantasies that can emerge with disappointment.

The Perspective Wheel also lets you take the 10,000-foot view. In the spirit of "What doesn't kill you makes you stronger," stepping back from tunnel vision makes it easier to see what positive things might come out of the situation, which makes it easier to make choices that are aligned with you at your best. You make fewer knee-jerk decisions.

Finally, the Perspective Wheel helps you come up with ideas you wouldn't have thought of from your Saboteur mindset. Sometimes, to jog the ideas, I ask clients to look at the problem from the perspective of their favorite childhood pet. It gets a chuckle and often shakes out something good.

THE PERSPECTIVE WHEEL, ADAPTED FROM CO-ACTIVE TRAINING INSTITUTE

1. Think of "the topic." Maybe it's your promotion, a difficult person at work, the direction of your career, or whether to get a pet cat.

CONFIDENCE AT WORK

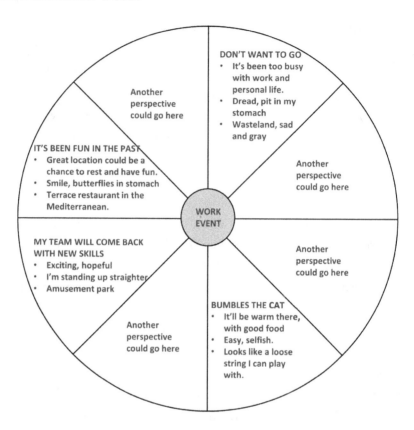

2. Put the topic in the middle of a large circle, then create 6-8 pie pieces. Each piece can contain one perspective.
3. Starting with one perspective:
   a. Write it in one piece of the pie: "I really don't want to go to that three-day work event."
   b. Describe it: "It's been a really busy period helping my teenager get into college, and I need a break."
   c. Experience how it feels in your body: "I feel dread, and it's showing up as a pit of anxiety in my stomach."
   d. Maybe imagine what landscape this perspective would be. "It looks like a wasteland, sad and gray."
4. Moving to another piece, write down another perspective.
   • "It's a bummer because I've had a lot of fun at these in the past. And they're always at fantastic locations, so you get some real R&R."

- "That perspective feels like a big smile on my face and butterflies in my stomach."
- "It looks like an outdoor restaurant overlooking the Mediterranean."

5. Keep doing this for up to six or seven perspectives. Remember, it's important to not mix the parts of you or your perspectives. Let yourself experience each one on its own.
6. Then, choose the perspective you **want** to **be in**. Not the "right" or "positive" one. Not the one you think others will find impressive or that your company will want you to choose. Choose the one **you** want to be in. You can decide on two, but don't choose them all because doing that will get in the way of clarity.
7. Then, write a to-do list from the perspective you've chosen. Hopefully, it's one you can be excited about or at least be motivated to get started on.

In the example above, taking action from the first perspective might make the person avoid their boss and create confusion. Brainstorming from the second perspective, they might come up with the idea to extend the trip and invite their spouse, and really recover from an exhausting stretch. Brainstorming from the perspective you want to be in aligns you with your Sage, and you begin to create that reality.

GETTING PERSPECTIVE ON FAILURE

It's important to remember that managing the Saboteur doesn't guarantee a perfect outcome every time. I really like the definition of four types of failure I learned from business coach Monica Shah of Revenue Breakthrough, which I'll paraphrase here:

1. Learning mistakes: Here, you know the vision and are on track. Still, you can't know everything before you do it, so when something goes wrong, you simply learn and keep going.
2. Course corrections: Here, what you learn from the mistakes you make leads you to make adjustments to the vision or the roadmap.

3. Holding a mirror: This level of course correction goes deeper. You may question the motives and/or the assumptions you and/or your team made. You may scrap the project, but if you continue it will be a major re-work.
4. Force majeure: Here, all bets are off. 9/11, the COVID-19 pandemic, and bankruptcy are all events that change reality and require deep reflection and entirely new solutions.

We've looked at several tools that can help you take initiative. Initiative matters because it is such an important part of gaining the experience that builds foundational confidence. There's a scene in Harry Potter where the kids have to conjure up their worst fear. One of them imagines an eight-foot-tall hairy spider. Then he waves his wand at it and says, "Ridiculous!" and the spider disappears with a "poof!" Learning to deal with the voice in your head is a powerful way to move forward through doubt, through the Facade, and into foundational confidence.

Saboteur: _____

What resonates about it: _____

In what situations does it mostly show up: _____

What does it do when I'm not around? _____

What threatens it: _____

How does it connect to my Social Style (extra): _____

CHAPTER 6
TIME MANAGEMENT FOR ENERGY, BALANCE, AND CONNECTION

At the start of the 2020 pandemic, people weren't very interested in personal growth; they were in mission-critical mode. Like many coaches, I wanted to help. Having worked from home for 15 years, where life and work blur, I realized there was one way I could help: time management. It turns out that the more flexibility you have over your time, the more behind the eight ball you can feel. Good time management helps build foundational confidence because it helps you get back to feeling on top of work and life.

There are times in your career, maybe early on when you are so focused and driven that you can work and work. Eventually, though, it becomes unsustainable. As your work evolves from individual contributor work, your career increasingly depends on motivating others, managing more complex tasks, and engaging in higher levels of strategic thinking and coordination. That transition requires shifting how and where you spend your time. What's more, working from home has made work seep into the mental load of personal time. As you evolve as a leader, it's easy to unconsciously sacrifice the things that are most connected to your well-being. Burnout and loss of a sense of purpose hurt confidence, and you become less effective.

The I to the 4th Power principles are related to time management in important ways. Focus, which my clients consistently express wanting, increases when you know what you bring to the table and have a sense of agency (Impact). Connection, which happens thanks to effective interactions and trust with colleagues (Influence), frees up energy you might be spending on interpersonal stress. Knowing how to manage the Saboteurs that knock you out of alignment helps maintain the Sage mindset (Initiative), which also frees up energy you can redirect towards reaching your goals. I revisit these principles here because they are foundational to this chapter. If those principles don't feel clear, then time management becomes a chore. If your Impact, Influence, and Initiative are clear to you, time management becomes a tool to increase your well-being and confidence.

START BY SHIFTING YOUR MINDSET

One of my absolute favorite exercises to do with individuals and teams is the Appreciative Inquiry I shared in Chapter 5. In my experience, most professionals are very productive, but they spend their time feeling behind the eight ball. Why? Because we are naturally fueled by the negativity bias—the Saboteur that tells you it's never enough—*you're* never enough. When, instead, you give mind, body, and soul that hit of satisfaction before going on to the next task, your mindset enjoys a game-changing shift.

Here is the exercise again:

1. What is the accomplishment?
2. Why is it important?
3. What would further progress look like?
4. What, if any, are the immediate next steps?

Another quick mental shift is to write down three things you're grateful for in the morning and evening. I shared this in the earlier chapter on Initiative, and it applies again here. Feeling on top of things doesn't just come when your work is done—it's the opposite. It's easier to get your work done when you approach it from a place of feeling good about yourself.

The next mindset shift I first learned about was from business coach Monica Shah in her *Breakthrough Planner: 90-Day System for Entrepreneurs*. First, decide *who* you want to be as you approach the next few months:

- "I am a trusted colleague to my co-workers."
- "I am skilled at what I do."
- "I am a future leader."

Then, when thinking about who you want to be, consider how you will support that identity: patient, open to listening, enthusiastic, accountable, engaged, etc. Connecting with your Sage confidence at the start makes planning and executing your plan much easier.

FOUR POWERFUL TOOLS TO MANAGE TIME AND BUILD CONFIDENCE

Here are the four tools that I've leaned into heavily over the years:

1. Limit yourself to three quarterly goals
2. Use a whole-life to-do list
3. Use the Eisenhower Matrix (Important, Not Urgent)
4. Schedule everything

LIMIT YOURSELF TO THREE QUARTERLY GOALS

Think about where you or your team would like to be in three years. This may include goals that are negotiated with your leadership, but it's important to take ownership. To do that, think about how to work toward that goal in ways that energize you and your team. Describe the experience. How many people will there be on your team in three years? How will people in the organization describe your team's culture? What will people say about the work you and your team produce? What does your team love about the vision and direction? How will customers (internal and external) describe working with you and your team? How will your team describe working with you? What accomplishment will your team be most proud of? What will you do better than anyone else?

Next, focus on one year. What do you need to have accomplished on today's date in 12 months to be on track to your longer-term vision? Spend time here to get this all down on paper; it might be a lot. If you and your team anticipate personal issues that could require focus, get those down, too. You are downloading ideas.

Now, prioritize the ideas by selecting just three for the next quarter. We can only handle a few areas of focus at once. Therefore, if you limit yourself to three quarterly goals, your overall progress will be much greater than if you let yourself work on 12 goals. This means that prioritizing three goals each quarter will get you further after six quarters than if you worked on 12 goals all the time.

It can be hard to deprioritize certain goals! Everything feels urgent. For seven quarters, I postponed updating my website because I had other, more urgent projects. For seven quarters, every time I looked at my website, I cringed. The enormous benefit of this ruthless cutting is that you do fewer things with more focus. You do them better, and you come up with more sophisticated solutions. The confidence you and your team feel makes future work better.

A note on the nature of goals. Should you create attainable goals or stretch goals? This is a good question. You have to know yourself. Some people love goals that take everything to the next level. So even if they don't reach their stretch goal, they feel satisfied that they upleveled the system and created real change on their way to the goal. Others prefer reachable goals that they can meet and exceed.

In the *Breakthrough Planner,* Monica Shah makes the next several suggestions: First, once you have decided on your three goals for the quarter, ask: Why is this goal important? What will it make possible for our department, team, or the organization? This important step makes you take ownership, which engages everyone.

Then, for each goal, you will have sub-goals. Here is where you define steps that will get you to the goal. So, for "Updating the website," you may have "Identify web designer and negotiate a contract," "Write copy," and "Review designer submissions and edit." Breaking things down into smaller pieces makes it easy to tick them off.

Sometimes, when you have more than three goals, you may realize that they roll up into one larger goal. So maybe you have to hire a new social media manager, update your website, and film a new company video. Depending on the size of your team, these are enough for one quarter, or they would be sub-goals that roll up into a larger "Uplevel Marketing" goal. The important thing is to have just three overarching goals with individual workflows so that your focus doesn't get fragmented and you stay on course.

Along with project goals, Monica points out that you will also have ongoing tasks. Account for these, as they take time. Think also about what obstacles you might encounter as you work toward the goals. Will a lot of team members take a vacation this quarter? Do some of your goals require support from levels above yours? Do others require training?

Finally, plan what you will do to celebrate your efforts. It's important that celebration not be attached to the outcome. You don't need to achieve the goal, especially a stretch goal, to celebrate your effort. I'm not advocating that you reward yourself for a mediocre outcome. I'm simply saying that when you work hard, even if you don't get the goal, you are learning and making an effort. Celebrating that is important for motivation. And, if you don't reach your goal(s), it is important to explore why. Were they realistic? Did you get redirected? How did you respond? These are important to explore.

USE A WHOLE-LIFE TO-DO LIST

Since first seeing the whole life to-do list in Stephen Covey's *7 Habits of Highly Effective People*, it has been one of my favorites. Several key features make it work. First, it doesn't separate work from personal. That doesn't mean you should sit at your work desk entertaining friends. But it does mean that you have permission to schedule a doctor's appointment in the middle of your workday if you know that they aren't open on the weekend. And yes, permit yourself to respond to work emails on Sunday morning for 30 minutes if doing that will declutter your mind and decrease your mental load.

The next feature of this to-do list is that you list tasks according to your role, always beginning with yourself. Some possible roles are "Team Leader," or "Project Manager," or "Analyst." You can also include personal roles that you play, "Parent," "Partner," "Son/Daughter," and "Friend." For each role, give yourself a goal for the week. Maybe you want more energy, so you write that in the "Self" section:

Self	Maintain energy	• Swim 2x
		• Walk 4x
		• Meditate 5x
		• Lunch with a friend 2x
Team Leader	Deliver Year-End Reviews	• Schedule time with each team member
		• Review assessments/prepare comments
		• Deliver reviews
		• Schedule follow up meeting with each report
Head of Sales	Prepare National Sales Meeting Speech	• Write rough draft
		• Consult with marketing, finance, and CEO
		• Check with event planner on tech and stage
Spouse/ Parent	Prepare for Holidays	• Buy gifts
		• Tip building staff
		• Select menu and food shop
		• Send out cards

There is tremendous focus when you keep a to-do list this way. As you do so, make sure to write the task in a way that makes sense. Too often, we write tasks that are much too big. So, "Get Promoted" becomes something that you can't get started on, and you move from list to list without chipping away at it. Instead, you might write, "Read a book about career strategy" or "Schedule time with a mentor or colleague who has been promoted." And later, "Identify key decision makers" and "Identify key accomplishments." Notice also that in each of these tasks, there is a verb that defines the movement of the task. If you write, "Key decision makers," it doesn't have the same flow as saying, "Identify key decision makers."

USE THE EISENHOWER MATRIX

The Eisenhower Matrix is often referred to as the "Important, Not Urgent Matrix. That's because Important, Not Urgent, is where the gold is.

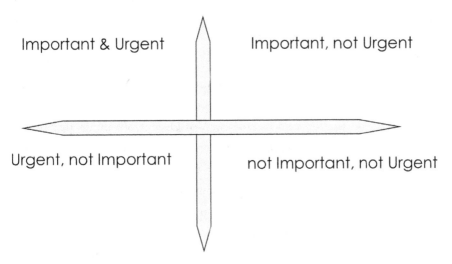

One of the key things most explanations of the Eisenhower Matrix don't highlight is that it's important to know where and how you add value. First, you add value using your core strengths, as we've discussed in this book. But you also add value in different ways at different levels. By this, I mean that your core strengths build with your experience, so you are leveraging them for a broader-reaching outcome. New managers often miss this and continue to do tasks that could be assigned to others. They overlook "thinking, strategizing, planning" tasks that are now required of them but that don't feel as immediately gratifying as individual contributor tasks. Once you are clear on what work you need to be doing, either from your own evaluation or from a conversation with your boss, you can start to use the Matrix.

First, the Important and Urgent quadrant. In this space, you put all of the critical things on your to-do list. These are the things that YOU need to do.

Ideally, around 60% of the work where you add value should show up here. Keep in mind that once you are a people leader, more of the people leadership tasks go into the Important and Urgent quadrant.

Then, critically, is the decision about where to go next. The right answer is to go to the Important, Not Urgent quadrant, where the growth and innovation projects live. It's also the quadrant where procrastination lives. That's because growth and innovation are inherently uncertain. Uncertainty triggers the saboteur in a big way. Things that live in the Important, Not Urgent, are sales and business development, operating systems that need to change, and difficult conversations. The trick is to schedule these things so you begin a chain of events: I have to train someone else to do some of the tasks I currently do, which naturally leads to delegation.

Other tasks that go into Important, Not Urgent, are things that have a due date of next week, next month, or next year. They are quite literally not urgent. Schedule them for when they are due so you can get them off your mind. One tip here. If something has a down-the-road due date, take time to evaluate whether the project requires set-up tasks. These are things like planning, assessing the workflows before they are assigned, conducting a kickoff meeting so the team is aware of the expectations for their involvement and deliverables, etc. Some of those pre-work tasks may then go into Important and Urgent.

Something interesting to be aware of is that the work we ignore or procrastinate often depends on our SOCIAL STYLE. Ideally, we get to focus mostly on the tasks that inspire us and that are in our areas of strength. But we all have to do things we don't like and/or that don't energize us. They may come easily to others but not to us. Still, they are necessary for the effective functioning of the team, and sometimes they fall to you. If that's the case, remember not to judge yourself for not liking it. Instead, give yourself a little extra grace, but do plan it and work on it.

Now we move to Not Important, Urgent. The key with this quadrant is that the task may be important to the project, the team, or the organization, but it's not important for YOU to be doing because *you need to delegate it*. Delegation is a big issue. If there's work that you know you need or want to stop doing, then setting someone else up for success in doing that work is a short-term project that needs to move from "Important, not Urgent" to "Important and Urgent." Make time for it. If you're saying, "I can get it done faster myself," you are misusing your precious time.

Finally, we have the Not Important, Not Urgent. The easy answer is that you should stay away from these tasks. The longer answer is that if you are spending too much time in this quadrant, consider whether you are experiencing burnout. If you are on social media, blowing off time at the water cooler, or getting caught up in gossip, then it may be time for a rest and recovery plan. The goal is to get back to the work that lives in the two "Important" quadrants. Those tasks are the ones that lead to your and your team's effectiveness and confidence.

SCHEDULE EVERYTHING

Scheduling everything has so many benefits that it's hard to know where to start. The first and most important is that it lets you declutter your mind by scheduling "Important, not Urgent things that aren't due today. When you work only from a single, daily to-do list, tasks tend to pile up vertically. That pretty quickly leads to overwhelm. Plan horizontally instead. Then, a task due in three weeks that will take a day or two to complete goes into your calendar for two and a half weeks from now. When you do that, you take the task out of your mental load, and that frees up space to focus on the tasks you're working on now.

The second thing scheduling everything does is that it allows you to cluster tasks. As I've gotten better at this, I can visually cluster my email inbox into categories: Client response, kids' school tasks, bill pay, phone calls, scheduling, and so on. Then, schedule 30 minutes or an hour to move through tasks that are similar to one another. When you do that, your brain isn't required to pivot as much. You are in the same context as you move through, and it takes less energy. And because it takes less energy, it is less likely to lead to procrastination.

The third way to use "schedule everything" is to reserve chunks of time. One of the biggest complaints I hear from clients is that they can't find chunks of time to do the "Important, Not Urgent" work they and their team need to do. Reserving chunks of time forces you to re-assign busy work that will interfere with those time chunks, or to move faster through tasks that eat up time. It's important not to slide back to doing the work you should be leaving to others.

The next reason to schedule everything is for self-care. Scheduling things you do anyway is a way to give yourself credit. If you make yourself lunch, schedule it. If you pop in to chat about a project with a colleague, schedule it, even if it's after the fact. There's nothing worse than getting to the end of the day, having spent time strategizing with a co-worker in an impromptu meeting, or calling three clients, and feeling like you haven't done anything because these things weren't on your original plan. Related to that, schedule time to restore throughout the day. If connecting with a colleague or friend is your thing, schedule a coffee break. Keep it short, but don't overlook it.

One critical key to scheduling everything is this. Be OK with adjusting the plan. If you think that going off plan is a sign of failure, it will only leave you feeling ineffective and unsuccessful. A plan is only a general outline. Adjusting is not a sign of failure; it's a necessary part of planning work. In *7 Habits*, Stephen Covey says that he had a favorite project manager who was great at his work. When Covey would assign this manager a task, he would say, "Sure, Mr. Covey, I'll do that, but then tell me what you're going to take off my plate." He had confidence, so he was OK with adjusting the plan. He didn't let the Saboteur make him think that saying "no" meant that he wasn't performing.

Time management that takes care of you has an important role in confidence. Remembering that when you are rested and ready and feel ahead of the eight ball, your Sage voice is strong. That is a huge confidence builder.

Chapter 7
LISTENING AND FEEDBACK THAT BUILD FOUNDATIONAL CONFIDENCE

"Seek first to understand, then to be understood."

—Stephen Covey

WHY AND WHEN TO LISTEN

Good listening is a virtue you hear about that has a range of benefits, including motivating your reports, promoting better collaboration on your team, and retaining your best talent. However, there are two applications of listening that I see as most closely related to building a sense of agency and foundational confidence:

1. Gaining context so you can respond more effectively
2. Providing difficult feedback

In this chapter, I will focus on those two situations and point you toward the ways in which listening intersects with the Social Styles and with the Saboteur.

LISTENING TO GAIN AWARENESS AND UNDERSTANDING

For my work, I am often asked to introduce myself in conversation. Before the intro, I almost always say, "I can tell you about myself in about 20 different ways. What would be most relevant?" or "What do you most want to know?" I don't say this to be rude, and I usually do it with a smile. What I know is that too often, we talk when we should be listening, and watching someone lose interest in what you're saying is a big confidence killer. The goal with listening first is to avoid going on and on as you watch your listener's eyes glaze over or see them check their watch.

Most of us talk because we think we are supposed to KNOW, to be the authority, or to somehow capture the listener's attention with our brilliance. What gets missed when you jump in and talk or solve is that people listen selectively. If, instead, you can take a moment to identify what your audience is most interested in, you can streamline what you're saying and keep their attention. This can be especially important with teams because you don't just lose their attention in that moment, you can dilute your credibility in the long term.

This approach to listening is a small but powerful shift that can serve you in many situations:

- Listening for clarification when problem-solving: You are working on a project, selecting from a range of possibilities on a sales strategy, or trying to get clarity on what a client wants. *Listening well to information from a range of perspectives lets you make more informed decisions.*

- Listening to engage and motivate: You want to engage or motivate someone. *When people feel heard, they are more comfortable taking more initiative. That, in turn, leaves you more time to get things done.*

- Listening to uncover hidden issues that could be putting everyone's hard work at risk: *Listening reduces tension, which makes people feel safe about sharing tough issues.*
- Listening to the feedback you're receiving: *You want people to feel comfortable offering feedback that they want to express.*

Listening well in your day-to-day work creates efficiency because everyone is more aligned, and you feel more confident.

HOW TO MOVE THE NEEDLE ON LISTENING

In her book *Guide to Interpersonal Communication*, my colleague Joann Baney references Robert Bolton's work, which defines three skill areas of active listening: Attending, Encouraging, and Reflecting. These skills, which I'll describe now, involve making the subject feel like the focus of your attention.

Attending Skills: Posture of involvement, eye contact, and a non-distracting environment.

Attending Skills are the skills we learn in primary school when the teacher says, "Pay attention, everyone!" A posture of involvement means that you sit up straight, square your shoulders, make eye contact, and put down the phone, book, TV, or any other distractions. In a work setting, finding a suitable environment usually means finding a quiet place with few distractions.

Important to Attending Skills is maintaining them. Not looking bored can be very important to the subject of your listening. If you are getting bored, take a moment to ask whether it's you or it's them. Are you bored because you feel like you already have the answer and feel it's a waste of your time to listen to other options? In that case, you may want to refocus and recommit to listening. If you are bored because this person has been repeating the same frustration for months, it may be an opportunity to challenge them.

Attending Skills are also a place to remember not to be so focused on your response that you forget to listen to the speaker. We think faster than people can talk, so it's easy to be so eager to move the conversation forward that you hijack what the subject says and weave it into your own narrative.

That can lead to people feeling talked over or feeling that you've stolen their ideas.

Encouraging Skills: Door openers, minimal encouragers, silence, and infrequent, open questions

Encouraging Skills are also natural, but most of us can benefit from using these skills with more awareness. What's important about Encouraging Skills is that you're not jumping in to express yourself or redirect the conversation. These small gestures let the speaker continue to hold the attention.

- Door openers are lines like, "Do you have a minute?" or "Can we talk about the issues on the client project?"
- Minimal encouragers use vocal and nonverbal communication like nodding, raising or furrowing their eyebrows, saying "Wow!" or "Sounds interesting," or "Tell me more." These are small nudges designed to let the subject continue what they are saying without significantly commenting on the content.

  Another powerful minimal encouragement is *acknowledgement*. When you can pepper the conversation with things like, "You really kept the team firing on all cylinders," or "What an interesting way to think about it," you validate the subject's thoughts and actions, and that creates a safe space.
- Silence and infrequent questions highlight that it's important to give someone the space to talk for a bit, whether they tend to talk a lot or a little. Infrequent questions are designed to help clarify a situation, not to offer an opinion. Sometimes, a yes/no question is appropriate. Other times, an open-ended question can help the subject deepen their expression of the situation.

  A yes/no question might be, "Just so I am clear, was only part of the team present?"

  An open-ended question might be, "What got in the way of everyone being there?"

Both types of questions are valid, though it's common to lean into yes/no questions when you have already come to a conclusion and are looking for confirmation. Open-ended questions can yield a broader scope of understanding. A broader scope can be important when feelings and opinions, not just facts, are an important part of the situation and the decision-making.

Reflecting Skills: Paraphrasing and summary statements

Reflecting Skills can be the most challenging. Paraphrasing asks you to repeat, often in the subject's own language or very closely paraphrase, what they said. It seems awkward at first, but usually, the subject doesn't notice; in fact, they feel seen and heard. Closing comments are lines you use to summarize the conversation like, "It sounds like your team has looked at a lot of options. What are the key takeaways?"

Attending, encouraging, and reflecting skills are powerful ways to make the person you are listening to feel seen and heard. In the language of the SOCIAL STYLE, it's a way to flex by focusing on reducing tension. Doing that is great because it builds trust, opens communication, and builds all-around foundational confidence.

DIFFICULT FEEDBACK (YES, CONFRONTATION)

Far and away, the topic that consistently sends a shiver up the spine of **I to the 4th Power** course participants is conflict. They want to know how to "deliver difficult feedback" without having the conversation go sideways. It's a critical skill to learn because simmering, unresolved conflict leads to a variety of problems: People can become protective or siloed, dragging others into their isolation. They can fail to create healthy boundaries, which diminishes self-esteem and confidence. Or they can become disengaged and leave the team or the organization. They suffer, and the work suffers.

The model for delivering difficult feedback is also originally from Robert Bolton's *Interpersonal Communication* (1979). The model has two stages:

CONFIDENCE AT WORK

1. The three-part message
2. Managing the response

THE THREE-PART MESSAGE

The three-part message: *"When you ... I feel ... because"* involves describing a person's behavior, expressing the feeling(s) that it creates in you, and explaining the effect on you.

"When you ..." is an objective statement of an observable action without judgment, editorializing, or assuming intention. An example might be, "When you leave your dishes and snack fixings on the counter ..." and NOT, "When you so rudely assume I'm here to be your housekeeper!..." This part is trickier than it looks; when we're upset, it's easy to jump to conclusions.

"I feel ..." is a statement that expresses the impact of the action on you. If "feel" is not a word that you want to use at work, you can say, "I get ..." or "I become ..." or just "I'm ..." For the example above, it might be, "I get discouraged ..." or "I get angry ..." Notice that the feelings can be different; different people can be affected differently by the same action. What's important about this part of the message is that it can feel vulnerable; you may not want to share how you feel. What's powerful about that, however, is that your feelings are your own; no one can deny them.

"Because ..." is where you provide a bit of background about your perspective. For the example above, it might be, "I get discouraged ...because after a long day at work, I have to clean the kitchen before I can start dinner." Or "I get angry ... because I've asked you to clean up after yourself before, and you said you would."

Some common work-related three-part messages might be:

"I notice you sent the report to Bob's office without letting me review it first. I'm confused. We've talked about this before, and I thought we were on the same page."

"The new assignment you gave me is for a much smaller part of the business. I'll be honest; it has me worried. Last year, I was promoted, and I thought I was doing a good job."

"It's the second time you've given short notice and left for vacation. I'm annoyed because our teams work so interdependently; when you do that, I have to scramble and re-do my team's workflows."

Having a structure for the message makes it easier. Next, you must manage the response.

MANAGING THE RESPONSE

When you deliver a three-part message, you should expect pushback. It would be wonderful if the response were, "Wow, I had no idea. Thanks for letting me know!" followed by a request for how you would like them to do things instead. Unfortunately, few people are wired that way. Delivering difficult feedback makes the tension between you and that person spike. When that happens, the typical responses will be to *deny, defend* or *deflect.*

Denial is when the person says it didn't happen or suggests that it wasn't what you thought you saw: "Oh, you must have misunderstood. I would never do that!"

Defensiveness is when they attack you back: "Your problem is that you don't like anything I do!"

Deflection is when they shift the focus to someone else or you: "The problem is with so-and-so. S/he is the one who leaves the mess in the kitchen!" or "I'm sorry you don't feel like you have a good relationship with Bob."

What's important at this stage is to realize that a spike in tension is normal. Just because the person has a strong and possibly negative reaction doesn't mean you've communicated incorrectly. From here, use active listening skills, specifically paraphrasing, to reduce the tension. Acknowledge what the person said, but stay calm and don't repeat any overly emotional words they've used. An example might be, "So, for you, the problem is my relationship with Bob." They may respond with "Yes!" That doesn't mean you've agreed and the conversation is over. It just means you are acknowledging what they've said.

The next step is to repeat your statement, exactly or closely. "The thing is, you sent the report to Bob's office before I could see it. I thought we were on the same page, so I'm a bit lost." The tension will rise again. This time, they may use a different strategy. Instead of deflecting onto the relationship with Bob, they may deny that anything is wrong, "You know what, I don't know what the problem is. None of the other managers mind when I take the initiative. It's only a problem with you." Again, use paraphrasing to reduce the tension. Then, repeat your feedback once more.

After a few cycles, the tension should break. Ideally, this will sound like, "OK, you know what? I get it. I'm sorry. I won't do it again." Often, it still carries some tension, "OK, fine. I get it!" Still, once there is acknowledgement of the issue, you can begin to problem-solve. Maybe the person says, "You know, it's hard for me to give you the reports because I get the data so late, and you are so thorough in your feedback. If you could read my reports faster, it would be easier. Can you do that?"

Building relationships and providing difficult feedback both improve when you listen well. To add even more nuance to the power of listening, consider how listening weaves in with Social Style and with the Saboteur.

LISTENING AND STYLES

For each of the skills of effective listening, there are opportunities to flex for each Style. When it comes to attending skills, consider that the tell assertive SOCIAL STYLEs, Driving and Expressive, will feel more at ease if you sit up, lean slightly forward, make eye contact, and use your hands more. The

Ask Assertive Styles, Amiable and Analytical, will be more at ease if you sit back slightly, have softer eye contact, and use your hands less. Expressive and Driving styles should be careful about being too direct, saying things like, "We need to talk!" or nodding excessively, which can intimidate or appear impatient. The Amiable and Analytical styles may want to be careful about being too laid back, which can come across as a lack of interest or judgment.

Encouraging skills also vary by SOCIAL STYLE. With minimal encouragers, what feels like an interruption to the Analytical and Amiable styles is viewed as positive verbal banter to the Expressive and Driving styles. Additionally, what feels like polite, poised listening to the Amiable and Analytical Styles can feel opaque to the Expressive and Driving; these Styles would like more feedback, both nonverbal and vocal. If you are on the Ask Assertive side, flex by being more reactive and using more minimal encouragement. If you are on the Tell Assertive side, flex by talking less and asking fewer questions.

LISTENING AND SABOTEURS

Saboteurs can have a powerful impact on listening. When your attending skills waver because you're nervous about your response in a meeting, that can be the Saboteur. When you take over a conversation because you feel like time's running out, that can also be the Saboteur. If it seems like the person you're listening to is getting sidetracked with emotional issues, that can also be the Saboteur.

Take a moment to revisit the Saboteur work you did in Chapter 5. If these thoughts come up while you are listening, it's another lens on your particular obstacles to being present for a conversation. When the feelings or thoughts do come up, revisit the active listening skills from this chapter. Find one or two adjustments you can make to listen better so you and the person you're listening to can be more comfortable, connected, and informed.

Managing listening and difficult feedback is so powerfully interconnected with communication and trust. Take the time to understand and practice these important tools. They will go a long way toward supporting you at your best.

CHAPTER 8
INNOVATION – BUILD YOUR TEAM'S CONFIDENCE AND LEVERAGE THEIR TALENTS

BUILD YOUR CONFIDENCE AS A LEADER, AND BUILD YOUR TEAM'S CONFIDENCE ALONG THE WAY

In my first job after business school, my new boss sat me down and shared her expectations. She gave me a list of behaviors that reminded me of a Girl Scout handbook. It included everything from "show up at work on time" to "never fudge your expense report." While it seemed basic, I loved the fact that she took the time to review it with me and that I knew where I stood.

In this chapter, you'll read about tools for engaging and mobilizing your team. It's a client favorite because, without a doubt, going from a skilled individual contributor to a newbie people leader comes with a big learning curve. Your confidence can take a hit. Most of us want to be good mentors and leaders, but many leadership models focus on the qualities of transcendent leaders like Jack Welch or Martin Luther King when what you need as a new leader are practical tools to help you manage the day-to-day. What's more, while some leadership principles are universal, remember that different people have different leadership styles. In Chapter 2, I mentioned the Change leader, the Vision leader, the People leader, and the Standards leader as four styles that correspond to the four Social Styles. Each of these Styles can be successful in leadership, and knowing how to adjust for your Style and the styles you have on your team is the key.

I once heard a TEDx talk by talented coach Susan Colantuono. Susan said that when senior leaders mentor their female reports, they tend to focus on encouraging these women to bring out the best in themselves and others; in short, to focus on relationships. When senior leaders mentor their male reports, they tend to focus on strategy and delivering results. Removing gender for a moment, I loved Susan's message because it focuses on *leadership and managing others as a strategy*. Innovation is the last of the four "I to the 4th Power" principles because, when your team feels confident, it encourages a safe space, and that's where strategic innovation becomes possible.

FIRST, ASSESS THE SITUATION

Many people jump into managing others without thinking about what they already have going for them. A great place to start is to look at your Social Style and then assess the situation:

- What strengths do you naturally bring to leadership?

    - Maybe you're good at positioning your team and their work to senior leadership.
    - Or you easily get everyone excited about the vision.
    - Maybe you bring out the best in everyone and know how to make them feel confident.
    - Or you understand processes, so you are good at keeping everyone moving through workflows.

- Where are your development opportunities that may impact the group?

- Maybe you could listen better, and sometimes you lose people as a result.
- Or you could be more systematic and less talkative.
- Maybe you are permissive with certain team members, which frustrates others.
- Or you get caught in the weeds and miss deadlines.

• If your team were a well-oiled machine, what would it look like?

- What will communication be like?
- How will your team deal with conflict?
- How will they celebrate?
- What will they want to take on next?
- What will they be known for?
- How will you be viewed by and influence the broader organization?

HAVE YOU EARNED THE RIGHT TO LEAD?

Different people have different ideas about what makes a good leader. If you've done the SOCIAL STYLE relationship map from Chapter 2 for your team, you can consider whether you've earned the right to lead from each person's perspective. A Driving Style employee might feel that "competent" is someone who consistently meets deadlines. For an Amiable Style employee, "competent" might mean that someone has deep connections throughout the organization and the ability to call in favors. Flexing to different styles enhances your right to lead people with different styles to yours.

Andrew Neitlich of the Coach Master Toolkit suggests several measures for assessing your leadership through others' eyes. These measures include *competence, credibility, personal commitment, integrity, resilience, serving others, commitment to employees' success, admitting mistakes, and modeling behavior.* Without becoming overwhelmed by the idea of being all things to all people, look for a few specific behaviors you could adjust to earn the right to lead with certain people.

> Nina was a high-potential middle manager who hired me because she wanted to break through to senior management. She had an impressive track record. She was an Analytical/Expressive combo, so she was super methodical but also fun and engaging. What made Nina an amazing boss was that she laid out a structured path for her direct reports and encouraged and celebrated them as they went along.
>
> Like most people, Nina didn't know how to appreciate her strengths because they came so naturally. At the start of our work, she said, "The problem is that I'm a generalist. I work in a financial services firm, but I'm not the best person here at any of the hard skills." Nina's challenge was a common one. I often call it the "mortar between the bricks" dynamic. When your strengths are in the soft skills/people side of things, they can feel hard to define. In reality, walls don't hold without the mortar. The key is to see and name what feels invisible. If you are good at getting people unstuck so they'll embrace system changes, that's important. If you can get a team motivated again after a disappointment, that's important, too if you are the one who synthesizes different elements of an initiative so that people work toward the same goal, again, super important.
>
> In short, Nina had earned the right to lead; in fact, it was her calling card, and she could pitch it to management. Nina had gotten several very well-prepared middle managers promoted within the organization. That was gold. Because she was methodical and detail-oriented, she was like a detective, finding places where those managers were getting stuck or where there were performance gaps to be closed. With that knowledge, she was able to talk about her impact. She could point to how improving the performance of the team she inherited had had an exponential impact on the bottom line. And in a well-articulated way, she could ask for assignments that would let her do the same, on a larger scale and with a new, more senior title.

EVALUATE THE TEAM'S TALENT

Looking at each person on the team, ask yourself, Who are the stars? Who needs support? Who may, unfortunately, not be a fit with your culture and goals? Assessing your team is not Machiavellian or opportunistic; it's a way to optimize the team. Think of the schoolteacher who is so distracted by an underperforming student that he or she doesn't have the time to support the ones who could really be stars. Or consider that as a team leader, you can get caught up with the people on your team who are easiest for you to get along with, and you don't invest the time to develop relationships with others. That can pretty quickly start to look like playing favorites.

Once you know who needs what, you can be more strategic about how to support each person and how to leverage their talents in service of results. Maybe you have a strong team member who could be taking more off your plate, working on special projects, or even training and mentoring more junior people. Maybe that person could benefit from guidance from a peer at your level in another department. Perhaps a redeployment of someone who is not working out, or worse, who is high-performing but toxic, can be a relief to other team members, who then perform better.

KNOW YOUR EMPLOYEES

People want career growth, and they want recognition. When you connect with each person's motivations and style, you recognize their talent and good work, and you can help them create a path to grow their career. Set up time to meet with each person. You'd be amazed at what you might learn. Again and again, I work with clients who tell me they haven't asked for a promotion but are hoping for one. What if someone on your team leaves because you didn't go to bat for them … because you didn't know they wanted a promotion?

For each employee, describe as much as you can about him or her. Ask them about their career and personal goals. Ask them what they want from their relationship with you. Ask them where they feel they contribute and where they would like to grow. One caveat here is that it's important to check with your organization's rules when asking about personal aspirations.

Asking a thirty-something woman if she wants to start a family is not a good or appropriate idea. But the more you can know about each person, the better you can lead them.

SET CLEAR EXPECTATIONS

Earlier, I mentioned my boss, who sat me down and shared her expectations for my approach to work. Expectations should not just be about what you want your reports to DO, but also how you want them to BE:

Being expectations

- How do you want them to communicate with you and others?
- How far do you want them to figure out an issue before they come to you for help?
- What kind of networks and relationships do you want them to develop in the organization?
- What do you want them to do or say in conflict situations?
- What "unwritten rules" in your team or organization do you want them to follow?

Doing expectations

- What do you want them to complete this quarter? This year?
- What projects or assignments will you ask them to take on?
- What skills or knowledge do you want them to acquire?

What they can expect from you

- How will you respond if things go wrong?
- If things go right?
- What will you do to help them grow in their career and leadership?
- How will you set the vision?
- How will you support them with challenges in work? In personal life?
- How frequently will you meet with them and provide feedback?

Remember to position expectations and growth opportunities as positive, next-level steps. The negativity bias naturally leads us to focus on what needs to be fixed. I've too often seen managers talk about growth goals as if the person should already know them and is failing to meet the goal. That can be quite discouraging. It may be obvious to you that a goal is positive but remember that the employee also has a negativity bias.

USING STORY

"The three-martini lunch is dead," I often say, which gets an eyebrow raised and a wry smile from course participants. What's good about that is that people aren't tipsy in the office during the afternoon. What's less good is that a lot of the organic mentoring that happened at those lunches is lost. Back in the day, lunch with the boss was an opportunity to hear war stories and to get advice. It was also a time when the boss could hear what was going on and get better aligned with the team.

Many of the leaders I work with forget the value of their experience, or they're just too busy. They are also usually focused on "what's still not done" and forget to stop and appreciate what they have learned along the way. Often, I experience clients feeling that it would be arrogant to assume they have the wisdom to pass on. But you do have wisdom, and your team can benefit from hearing it.

Andrew Neitlich again shares some good suggestions for stories to share: Overcoming a challenge or adversity, learning from a failure, key lessons about being a better leader, how a team came together despite difficult circumstances, the best leader you ever worked with, and what you learned, the worst leader you ever worked with and what you learned, insights about your own shortcomings and how you overcame them, how the organization has evolved and where it is headed, someone you know who learned a key lesson that is relevant to your work, and on and on. Find opportunities to share stories, even if they are short versions. If they are short and memorable, your team can, in turn, use them to train their own direct reports.

CELEBRATE THE WINS

The Strengths Finder model emphasizes that positive acknowledgments have the greatest impact on employee engagement. A simple way to do that is to use the Appreciative Inquiry tool that I've mentioned more than once. Articulate the accomplishment, then share why you think it's important. As a bonus, let the person know what's possible (i.e.-further progress) because of what they did. Or, you can use the "When you…I feel…because…" with a focus on something positive. Remember also that different people want to be acknowledged in different ways. Some want public acknowledgement, like a party or a mention in a meeting. Others want privileges, like access or visibility. And as you link consistent wins and positive performance to rewards, don't just limit yourself to raises and promotions. Most companies have many resources, like tuition reimbursement, events, or special projects.

I hope that this chapter pulls back a curtain on one of the management parts of leadership so that you can feel confident as you take it on. Often, leaders spend their time trying to be an impressive tower of knowledge about the work the team is doing, and they miss the fact that managing the day to day is key to good leadership. When you take the time to be a good people manager/leader, your team is connected, aligned, and consistently able to give their best. You get to feel confident with them and with the feedback you hear from the broader organization.

CHAPTER 9
INNOVATION – CREATING SPACES FOR IDEAS TO EMERGE

Chapter 8 discussed tools to help your team break the confidence Facade and begin to invent their own authentic, foundational confidence. An important complement to individual development is to examine and understand team dynamics. In today's competitive, fast-changing environments, you need the talents of each team member, *plus* the edge that comes from effective collaboration. In the end, that collaboration is the glue that generates the magic.

There are three models I've relied on over the years:

1. The SOCIAL STYLE as a team functioning model. I've talked about the SOCIAL STYLE Model at length. I would invite you to revisit Chapters 2 and 3 and consider how different talents, perspectives, and energies contribute to making a team or a project successful.
2. The Direction/Alignment/Commitment model and the Dependent, Independent, and Interdependent models from the

Center for Creative Leadership. These tools are fantastic because they are so simple. I'll go into them more in this chapter.
3. The Five Dysfunctions of a Team Model by Patrick Lencioni. I love it because it provides a framework for human emotion and ego aren't always measured with team dynamic models that focus exclusively on roles and responsibilities.

THE CENTER FOR CREATIVE LEADERSHIP DAC MODEL

The Direction/Alignment/Commitment model from the Center for Creative Leadership is simple to remember and offers a 10,000-foot view of effective teamwork. It's a great framework to use when preparing a year-end review, a team strategy, or a business model or plan.

Direction refers to agreement on the vision and the roadmap to get there.

- *When a team has strong direction:* Team members agree on the vision and roadmap.
- *When a team has weak direction:* Team members can be working at odds with one another.

Alignment refers to how the group coordinates different aspects of the work so that it serves the shared vision.

- *When a team has strong alignment:* Team members coordinate their work.
- *When a team has weak alignment:* There can be silos, duplicated efforts, or efforts at cross purposes.

Commitment refers to shared responsibility and seeing personal success as an outcome of team success.

- *When a team has strong commitment:* Team members maintain trust, even through ups and downs.

- ***When a team has weak commitment:*** Individual team members put their own interests first, especially when things are hard.

When these three elements pull a team in the same direction, the team has built foundational confidence at the collective level. There are fewer headwinds, the team is more effective, and authentic collaboration keeps them moving.

THE DEPENDENCE - INDEPENDENCE - INTERDEPENDENCE MODEL

To describe team dynamics and culture, the Center for Creative Leadership adapts the idea of the Dependent, Independent, and Interdependent pyramid I first read about in Stephen Covey's *The 7 Habits of Highly Effective People* to teams. In describing individuals, Covey said that Dependent individuals are in the "You" paradigm, relying heavily on the direction of others. This can be children, people who abuse substances, or who, for other reasons, don't have a strong sense of self. Independent individuals rely only on themselves and don't seek others' input to make decisions. They are in the "I" paradigm. Interdependent individuals are in the "We" paradigm. They do have a strong sense of self, and they are open to growing by considering other perspectives and input.

For teams, the Center for Creative Leadership describes these dynamics as follows:

Dependent leadership: People in authority are responsible for leadership
Independent leadership: Leadership emerges out of individual expertise
Interdependent leadership: Leadership is a collective activity

In *Dependent* teams, things may look like they're getting done, but capacity is bottlenecked by the boss. The team's creativity and capacity to innovate are buried. *Independent* teams can also look productive. They often have strong leaders at the head of each function. However, there are often silos and pressure for employees to be loyal to one or another leader. *Interdependent* teams enjoy a much greater flow of creative thinking and innovation. The heads of each function are aligned and committed to one another and are working towards a shared vision and purpose. People at any level can speak up, challenge one another, and grow within the team or beyond. These teams consistently keep up with or outperform changing market dynamics.

FINDING OPPORTUNITIES TO IMPROVE TEAM DYNAMICS

Many people don't like the title *The Five Dysfunctions of a Team* because it sounds negative. However, the benefit of looking at a team from this perspective is that "best practices" are often hard to see. Lencioni points us toward observable dynamics that most of us see every day.

Lencioni very effectively illustrates the elements of his model using a pyramid. Trust is at the foundation because it is subtle but broad in its scope. When trust wavers or is absent, people are not willing to be *vulnerable*. That leads to *Artificial Harmony* – everything might look fine, but team members don't speak up because they are afraid of conflict. Without clarity or transparency, there is a lack of commitment, which leads to *Ambiguity*. You then have a team that is not willing to hold one another accountable, which results in *Low Standards*. And finally, you have leaders who put themselves

first, which means there is an inattention to results. They are focused on their own *Status and Ego*, and they often have one foot out the door.

The goal, instead, is to encourage trust, be willing to listen to other points of view, and have norms for conflict that respect each team member. With clarity, everyone can commit; even if they have a different idea, being heard lets them have a choice about commitment. Team members hold one another accountable and put the vision ahead of their own interests. When you achieve these things, leadership stops being about the person at the top, and control is dispersed throughout the team.

PUTTING THE "I" BACK IN TEAM

For years, I've been saying, "We need to put the "I" back in TEAM as a correction to the overused mantra, "There's no 'I' in team!" As the dynamics I've outlined in this book have made work and life less and less certain for individuals, it's been harder for them to feel supported. In an effort to access the synergy that happens in a high-performing team, sometimes individual team members have gotten lost. When, instead, people feel heard and their ideas considered, I believe they can commit to another direction than their preferred one because they trust that the team is in it together. When you can free your team of the friction that comes from a lack of commitment, performance can grow exponentially.

CHAPTER 10
WHERE DO WE GO FROM HERE?

We're facing a time of unprecedented uncertainty and chaos that requires confident leaders, secure in their ability to rise to the moment. Confidence at Work has laid out a blueprint for finding success as your authentic self, even when you, your employees, or your entire company are faced with uncertainty.

Authentic, foundational confidence matters because you don't serve yourself, your future, or your company by showing up with anything less than the full impact you are capable of creating, even in the most challenging circumstances. The confidence you can develop through applying the ideas and exercises in the I to the 4th Power system, will not only lead you to greater success and achievement but to find fulfillment every step of the way.

Ultimately, my leadership Style has me most interested in vision. What I love about vision is that it can so powerfully energize people to solve big challenges and achieve big goals. And every word in this book is designed for you to experience this for yourself.

It's hard to know exactly what's going to happen next. As we find solutions to issues of climate change, inequity, and political division, I believe businesses can have a leadership role rather than be regulated into compliance. I believe that individuals and teams with authentic, foundational confidence are critical to getting us to a more positive outcome. As Shirzad Chamine says, we can create the future from fear, stress, anger, guilt, shame, and insecurity, or we can create it from empathy, curiosity, creativity, passion, and purpose.

While senior leadership sets the goals, it is the middle managers, for whom this book is written, who will do so much of the work to get us there. They'll make it happen not just because they are following orders but because they, too, are granted the autonomy to take risks and share ideas. Solving the world's biggest issues right now can't happen without the creative force of everyone in the organization.

It's time to take this energy out into the world:

- **Impact** so you can leverage your talents and those of others for extraordinary results
- **Influence** so you can feel confident in everything you do and find the effectiveness that comes from powerful collaboration
- **Initiative** so you can push through mediocrity and emerge brilliant and capable
- **Innovation** so you, your team, and your organization can thrive even in the most challenging moments.

Your team needs your talents, your company needs your talents, and the world needs your talents. When you can shift the Confidence Invention from being a facade to being authentic and foundational, your newfound confidence fuels the future.

WORKS CITED

Chapter 2
Tracom, Social Style. www.tracom.com
Strengths Finder 2.0. https://www.gallup.com/cliftonstrengths/en/252137/home.aspx

Chapter 5
Achor, Shawn. *The Happiness Advantage,* Currency, imprint of Crown Publishing Group, division of Penguin Random House LLC, New York.
Shamine, Chirzad. *Positive Intelligence,* Greenleaf Book Group Press, Austin, TX, 2016
Filipe Rocha
Co-Active Training Institute. www.coactive.com

Chapter 6
Covey, Stephen. *The 7 Habits of Highly Effective People.* Free Press, division of Simon & Schuster. New York, 1989
Shah, Monica. *Breakthrough Planner.* Monica Shah, 2023

Chapter 7
Baney, Joann. *Guide to Interpersonal Communication.* Pearson Education Inc., New Jersey, 2004

Chapter 8
Neitlich, Andrew. *CoachMaster Toolkit,* www.wbecs.com

Chapter 9
Center for Creative Leadership. www.ccl.org
Lencioni, Patrick. *Five Dysfunctions of a Team,* Josey-Bass, a Wiley Imprint, San Francisco, 2002

www.ingramcontent.com/pod-product-compliance
Lightning Source LLC
Chambersburg PA
CBHW070847150125
20234CB00009B/196